AF621995

What to do when your child hates school

What to do when your child hates school

Antonia Chitty

Viva Books
New Delhi | Mumbai | Chennai | Kolkata
Bangalore | Hyderabad | Kochi | Guwahati

Copyright © Antonia Chitty

First Indian Edition 2010

VIVA BOOKS PRIVATE LIMITED

- 4737/23 Ansari Road, Daryaganj, New Delhi 110 002
  E-mail: vivadelhi@vivagroupindia.net, Tel. 42242200
- 76, Service Industries, Shirvane, Sector 1, Nerul, Navi Mumbai 400 706
  E-mail: vivamumbai@vivagroupindia.net, Tel. 27721273, 27721274
- Jamals Fazal Chambers, 26 Greams Road, Chennai 600 006
  E-mail: vivachennai@vivagroupindia.net, Tel. 28290304, 28294241
- B-103, Jindal Towers, 21/1A/3 Darga Road, Kolkata 700 017
  E-mail: vivakolkata@vivagroupindia.net, Tel. 22836381, 22816713
- 7, Sovereign Park Apartments, 56-58, K. R. Road, Basavanagudi, Bangalore 560 004
  E-mail: vivabangalore@vivagroupindia.net, Tel. 26607409, 26607410
- 101-102 Mughal Marc Apartments, 3-4-637 to 641, Narayanguda, Hyderabad 500 029
  E-mail: vivahyderabad@vivagroupindia.net, Tel. 27564481, 27564482
- Beevi Towers, First Floor, SRM Road, Kaloor, Kochi 682 018, Kerala
  E-mail: vivakochi@vivagroupindia.net, Tel: 0484-2403055, 2403056
- 232, GNB Road, Beside UCO Bank, Silpukhuri, Guwahati 781 003
  E-mail: vivaguwahati@vivagroupindia.net, Tel: 0361-2666386

www.vivagroupindia.com

Published by arrangement with

Crimson Publishing,
a division of Crimson Business Ltd
Westminster House, Kew Road
Richmond, Surrey TW9 2ND

All rights reserved. No part of this book may be reproduced or utilized in any form or by any means, electronic or mechanical, including photocopying, recording or by any information storage or retrieval systems, without permission in writing from the publisher.

This edition is for sale in the Indian subcontinent only. Not for export elsewhere.

ISBN : 978-81-309-1487-9

Published by Vinod Vasishtha for Viva Books Private Limited, 4737/23, Ansari Road, Daryaganj, New Delhi - 110 002.

Printed and bound by Raj Press, R-3, Inderpuri, New Delhi - 110 012.

Contents

Introduction

The school years can be challenging for parents and children alike. If your child is struggling, you may have problems working out how to help. If your child is playing up or behaving badly, it can be hard to understand that they may be trying to tell you something. However, you're not alone. Your child's problem may seem unique, but there's probably another mother or father who has been through something similar. This book will help you to help your child through a range of issues. Read on to find out how other parents have helped their child cope with academic challenges, bullying and other problems at school. You will also find tips from experts and useful resources.

Where to start

If you think the school isn't meeting your child's needs, start with Chapter 1. There is lots of information to help if you want to work out whether your child has special educational needs, and how to access additional help, with example letters to make it easier to follow what can be a complex process.

If your child is struggling at school due to traumatic events such as bullying, serious family illness, death or divorce, Chapter 2 is full of useful information. Chapter 3 will help you work problems out with the school, starting with informal meetings and guiding your through more formal complaints procedures to the head and to Governors. There are also contacts if you need to go further.

If you have got to the stage where it no longer seems possible to work things out with your child's current school, Chapter 4 will fill you in on your options when changing school. From following the process to move within the state system, to explanations about all sorts of independent schools, this chapter makes it clear where to go next. And Chapter 5 takes things one step further if you feel your child needs a break from school, and you would like to look into home educating, flexischooling and tutors.

Some problems can affect children of all ages, while other issues crop up mainly at secondary school. Chapters 6 and 7 look at children aged 11 to 16 and 16-plus respectively, dealing with academic and career issues, as well as looking at online and phone bullying, racist and homophobic bullying.

Chapter 1

From special needs to academic issues

Why do children have problems with school? There's no single answer to this one as the issues vary from child to child. This chapter looks at some of the reasons children learn at different rates, how conditions like Asperger's, dyslexia and autism can affect your child at school, and the help you can get. We also examine why bright kids may have problems at school too, and how to help. See Chapter 2 for more on bullying, truancy and how events in the family can cause stress at school.

IS YOUR CHILD STRUGGLING TO KEEP UP?

Some children take longer than others to learn, or may struggle with schoolwork or behaviour. It can be hard to know when to look for more help and advice, or whether to just accept that some children learn more slowly than others. Professor Patricia Preedy has 12 years' experience as a head teacher at a beacon school and also has, among other qualifications, a Masters in Educational Management investigating how schools can work in partnership with parents. She says, "Children can have some sort of learning difficulty, which may not emerge initially. As they get older it can become evident that their peers are 'taking off' whilst they are making slower progress. This frequently becomes evident at around the age of six but may also happen at later key stages."

Things to eliminate

Firstly, it is worth eliminating physical issues such as poor hearing or sight. Ask your GP or school nurse about getting your child's hearing checked. Professor Preedy says, "I assessed an 11 year old and we were all surprised to find out that he could barely hear in one ear." Shortsightedness becomes more common as children progress through secondary school and can easily go unnoticed. All children are entitled to free NHS eye examinations. Ask friends if they can recommend a local optometrist to check whether your child might need spectacles.

If you do find your child has problems with sight or hearing, tell the teacher as soon as possible. Even if you are waiting for hearing aids or spectacles to be made up, the teacher can make sure your child is sitting in the best position for them, and take a little extra time to check they are keeping up.

Professor Preedy advocates thinking about other possible causes of delayed development, saying, "Think about whether birth problems or early childhood illnesses could have impacted on your child. A child who was born prematurely could find themselves effectively in the wrong year group. When they get older this won't have such a big impact, but at age four a few months' difference is a large proportion of your life."

Help from the school

If your child's sight and hearing are fine, ask to speak to the

SENCO, the person who is responsible for co-ordinating help for children with special education needs. They should have experience of children with a range of abilities and be able to look at your child's progress. Ask whether they think your child has difficulties, or special educational needs. Find out if your child is working at the same level as children of a similar age, or whether the SENCO and class teacher think they could do with further assessment or extra help. They may suggest devising an Individual Education Plan (see below).

If your child has special educational needs, the school has a duty to meet their needs and provide them with 'a broad, well-balanced and relevant education'. In most cases your child's education will be in a mainstream school, perhaps with outside help from specialists. For a few children a specialist school may be more appropriate.

What sort of help?

There is a staged process for bringing in more help for a child with additional educational needs, using internal and possibly external specialists. Throughout this process, the school must listen to you and your child, consult you, and take into account what your child wants. The SENCO can help you through the process. They are not there necessarily to provide all the extra input themselves, but can arrange for the help your child needs.

THREE STEP PLAN

There are official terms in England for three steps in getting your child the help they need:

1 School Action: This is the stage when you and the school decide

your child needs more help. Progress should be monitored, and if the extra support is not making enough difference you move on to...

2 School Action Plus: The class teacher or SENCO will talk to you about getting more help from someone outside the school. This could be an educational psychologist, a speech and language therapist or simply a specialist teacher.

3 Statement of Special Educational Needs: If your child needs still more help to make progress, you need to start thinking about applying for a Statement of Special Educational Needs.

ENQUIRE

In Scotland, Enquire provides advice and help for parents and young people about additional support for learning. You can call them on 0845 123 2303 or visit **www.enquire.org.uk** to download an excellent and comprehensive guide to additional support for learning in Scotland.

What can help at school

To start with, the school should offer to look at different ways of teaching that work well for your child. They may benefit from extra input from a teacher or assistant, focussing on work they find harder. Or the school may arrange special equipment which will help them meet your child's needs. The school should keep you informed about this and any other actions that they take. Their plans for your child should form an Individual Education Plan. This plan helps everyone who works with your child know their weaknesses and strengths, and which strategies work well for them. Once this is set up, book regular meetings to talk about your child's progress. You may want to meet every term or more often if issues arise.

Help at home

You will probably be able to help your child at home, alongside whatever the school is doing. Talk to the SENCO or class teacher and ask them about what you can do to help your child practise the things that they struggle with.

Outside help

The SENCO can also tell you how to get referred for external help from, for example, a speech therapist or other professional. You may find it useful to ask the local education authority about your local parent partnership service, which can provide you with help and support.

Educational psychologists

You may come across an educational psychologist if your child receives an assessment for special educational needs. The local authority employs educational psychologists to check your child's progress at school. Educational psychologist Tim Francis says, "An assessment will involve taking your child's developmental history. An educational psychologist will look at levels of reading, writing, spelling and comprehension. He then makes recommendations for an 'intervention' – in other words he suggests how best to help your child." The assessment may involve talking to other professionals involved with your child. You can also go to an independent educational psychologists and pay for an assessment.

Local education authority assessment of SEN

You can request an assessment for your child from the local authority. This assessment could lead to your child having a 'Statement of Special Educational Needs'. In Scotland you can ask for a Co-ordinated Support Plan, which is similar. According to government advice website Direct.gov, very few children actually need an assessment. The assessment is only offered if your child's school cannot provide all the help they need. The school may also ask for the assessment but should discuss this with you first. Some parents feel that their child needs a statement because their needs aren't being met, yet have to battle to get one. Senior Early Intervention Teacher Victoria Dawson says, "You, the parent, need to apply in writing which can be off-putting. Look for a template to help you."

To the Additional Educational Needs Manager
Your Local Authority

Dear *(Name)*
Re: *Your child's name (Date of birth) School*

I am writing to ask the Local Authority to carry out a Statutory Statement of Special Educational Needs for my child under the Education Act of 1996 as I am entitled to.

Or

I am writing to ask the Local Authority to carry out an assessment for a Co-ordinated Support Plan under the Education Additional Support for Learning (Scotland) Act of 2004 as I am entitled to.

Write in details of: your child's difficulties at school, other problems, medical history and diagnosis. Write down the help your child is getting already, for how long each day/week, and from whom. Then explain how this is not meeting your child's need. Back this up with evidence of slow progress.

Yours sincerely

Six-week wait

It can take up to six weeks for the local education authority to decide if they will do an assessment, and they must write and explain if they decide against your request. Talk to the school about how else your child's needs can be met if this is the case. You can also appeal to the independent Special Educational Needs and Disability Tribunal.

Richard was being home educated, due to bullying, but wanted to try school again. Mum Nicola asked for a Statement of Special Educational Needs as he has Asperger's Syndrome, to ensure that Richard's needs could be met by a new school. She says, "We got support from Families First who are there to support families experiencing difficulties, and were happy to support us in going for the statement that we felt that Richard would need to return to school. It was a little more difficult because usually statements are done through the school, with teachers' feedback etc, but we got statements from the Families First support worker and also from a local autism charity worker who had had experience with Richard attending various activities they organise for young people on the autistic spectrum.

"Richard is very academically capable but struggles a bit with some of the school set-up and noise. He now has full support at school. This is really hard to get, not least because of the cost. I feel we were successful in getting the level of support he needs. He's doing very well back at school and enjoying it for the most part. He's even been picked for the rugby team."

Professional opinions

If they do assess your child, they will get information on your child from the school, a doctor, and educational psychologist, social services if they know your child already, and any other relevant professionals. You can go to any part of the assessment with your child. You may want to suggest other people or organisations who should be involved in the assessment.

Report time

Once the information has been collected, the SEN officer decides whether to write a report. They will let you know this within 12 weeks of the start of the assessment. If the officer is not going to write a report, the local education authority should explain this decision, and how your child's needs can be met.

What is in a statement

If the local education authority decides to provide a statement of your child's needs, it will outline these needs and specify the help your child should get. It will also spell out the long-term aims for the help and the arrangements for regular short-term goals and reviews of your child's progress. The statement should also describe other, non-educational, needs and how these can be met. You get a chance to look at a draft statement and comment. Victoria Dawson says, "Once a year, you should be invited in for an Annual Review. This is your chance to review whether the statement is still meeting your child's needs."

Changing schools

As part of meeting your child's needs, the local authority will send you details of local state mainstream and special schools as well as independent schools that are approved by the Secretary of State for Education and Skills as suitable for children with SEN. You can visit the schools and check out whether they support the needs of your child. Around six in every ten children with special needs attend a mainstream school. Specialist schools may have facilities for helping children with different types of SEN, such as physical disabilities or dyslexia. You can say whether you prefer a mainstream school or special school.

The local authority has to agree with your preference as long as the school is suitable for your child's age, ability, skills and SEN. They also take into account whether your child's presence will damage the education of other children already at the school and be an efficient use of the authority's resources. The local authority does not have to fund your child at an independent school if there is a suitable state school place available.

Educational psychologist Tim Francis says, "After an assessment, most schools will implement the suggested intervention. However, a minority have no confidence, competence or interest in special needs. In this case you may want to look at the other schools available that are more supportive before starting on a fight with the school. Don't be deterred by a school's external appearance, but look inside to see how they welcome and support children with special educational needs." Tim is part of the team behind the website **www.educational-psychologist.co.uk** which is packed with articles on different topics to help you help your child.

Carolyn's son Gabriel has had developmental problems since he was born prematurely. She says, "He was late achieving all targets like walking, talking, potty training, etc. In school he was considered nice and polite but with a tendency to be easily distracted and unable to concentrate on lessons. At the junior school, age seven, his gains deteriorated. This school was more competitive and, basically, if the child was not causing problems then his needs weren't seen as a priority. My son couldn't keep up. He would come home from school pinch-faced and unable to remember what had happened on any given day.

One day he reported to me that the SEN teacher had done a very theatrical yawn when he was trying to read for her, then looked at her watch and said something like 'Come on I haven't got all day!' At the end of the year his teacher said he had only achieved about a third of where he should be over the year. I talked to the teacher, tried to get an appointment with the SEN teacher but we never managed it. I kept being told he was behind but making progress and not to worry. They didn't seem that bothered about him. He was a problem, but not a big one for them. The reality was that he wasn't improving and wasn't engaging but it wasn't until the end of the school year that they actually admitted that what they were doing hadn't worked. It was obvious that the school wasn't going to ever work for him and I had to do something drastic. I mentioned to the teacher about looking at other schools and she said she thought it was a good idea.

"I looked into private education. The local Steiner had a good reputation and I knew Waldorf Steiner education had a different perspective on child development. I strongly felt that in the right environment my son would be able to learn. There was a good feeling in the school. Location and cost played a part. They have a sliding scale of fees and I could just about manage the costs and the school is only about a mile away and as I don't drive I needed to be practical. After that visit I noticed some older kids outside the school sitting on some grass talking. They looked like kids from any school and I asked them what they thought of Steiner. Not one was sullen or rude or shy, they all said it was great and they loved it. I really didn't expect a group of teenagers to talk about their school that way.

"The emphasis on learning in a holistic way really helped my son develop an interest in learning again. There are no exams until they are 16 so there is less pressure on children and teachers to jump through arbitrary hoops. There is consistency too, with having the same teacher every year and building up that bond and trust. I think that has added to his sense of responsibility not to let his teacher or his classmates down and to try hard. He has developed a healthy competitiveness he never had before. The range of things they are doing allows him to find skills he might never had noticed. For example, he is really good at needlework and really impressed the crafts teachers with his eye for design. He has also developed a skill for storytelling and has been asked to develop a performance with his best friend for a special event.

"I really believe that an environment where being good at Art is treated as just as important as being good at maths has been really significant to him. My son, who struggled in fear with maths and English and is now considered average to the rest of the children in the class in maths and with his reading and handwriting, is for the first time making really steady, significant progress. Last week I met with his class teacher and his SEN teacher and they both are very pleased with his progress. He is happy too and enthusiastic about trying new things. He has had his normal ups and downs with friendships and schoolwork but seems to have found his niche."

SPECIFIC DIFFICULTIES

In this section, you can find out more about some of the most common causes of difficulties at school and how to help:

- Specific Learning Difficulties (dyslexia, dyspraxia, dyscalculia, attention deficit disorder)
- Autistic Spectrum and Asperger's Syndrome disorders
- Moderate Learning Difficulties
- Behaviour, emotional and social difficulties
- Gifted and talented

SIGNS OF DYSLEXIA

Children with dyslexia can be reluctant to go to school, or may have been labelled as disruptive. While there are no exact criteria for distinguishing dyslexia, there are some traits which the British Dyslexia Association lists as common to many children with the condition. In general, they will have 'good' and 'bad' days, for no apparent reason, and often confuse directional words, such as up and down, in and out. Dyslexic children will have difficulties with sequences, such as putting coloured beads into a pattern, and remembering days of the week or numbers. There may also be a family history of reading difficulties. For more detailed lists of signs to watch out for, see the British Dyslexia Association's website: **www.bdadyslexia.org.uk**.

> Jennifer's son Alex seemed different from other children right from when he started nursery. She says," He didn't want to paint or draw like the other children. However, it only became a problem once he started school. We fought for years, arguing with school, the local authority and educational psychologists to have him recognised as having Special Educational Needs. His teachers just said he was being difficult or arrogant or lazy. Educational psychologists said his difficulties weren't that severe and the local authority said they didn't have any money in the budget. We had meeting after meeting with teachers: they were rarely

helpful and ultimately we ended up just telling them to leave him alone. We felt they were bullying him, and his behaviour in class was getting worse and worse, yet he was still a pleasure to be with at home."

In the end Jennifer took Alex to a private educational psychologist, who identified him as having severe dyslexia. The family used the report successfully, after some battles, to insist that the local authority provided for him. Jennifer arranged for extra lessons for Alex to help him keep up. She says, "Once the local authority provision was in place he had lessons at a Special Unit. Some people thought that it would be a negative taking him out of school for this provision, but it helped him when he needed the space outside the school environment. Later he had a Special Needs Tutor who came into school to help him and they developed a very good relationship."

Alex had become ostracised from his class and one teacher concentrated on reintegrating him. Jennifer says, "This worked well. She recognised his visual spatial skills and put him as leader of a group."

"When he went to high school we persuaded them not to put him into the Moderate Learning Difficulties class, as he would cause problems with his behaviour if he was not stimulated. Although he struggled with the work he was bright. They really were not sure but we were insistent and eventually they agreed to put him into the 'top class' as a trial. He stayed there throughout school, became Head Boy and left with eight GCSEs, which he sat with maximum provision of extra time and a scribe to write for him."

The family found that the secondary school was very helpful. Jennifer says, "Although they couldn't provide a great deal in the way of tuition because of lack of resources, their attitude toward him was positive and that made a lot of difference. Ultimately, our greatest support came from the SEN co-ordinator at High School and from the local authority."

Now 23, Alex has a job he loves for a small family company who value his skills and strengths, and understand the areas where he will always struggle. He has just bought his first flat and is happily settled with his girlfriend.

DYSGRAPHIA AND DYSCALCULIA

Most people will have heard of dyslexia, but if your child struggles more with writing or maths, you may want to investigate dysgraphia or dyscalculia. Signs of dysgraphia include illegible writing and poor spelling in an otherwise bright child. Similarly, if your child finds it difficult to do mathematical calculations, and doesn't notice that they frequently reverse numbers, they may have dyscalculia. This may not mean that they are poor at all things mathematical, but could have problems with specific areas such as remembering times tables or formulas, reading and understanding maths questions, or laying out their answers in the way the teacher wants. Educational psychologist Tim Francis explains, "A child with dysgraphia may be helped if they learn to touch type and are given a laptop. A child with dyscalculia may benefit from a multi-sensory approach, like doing their sums in a sand tray or using play dough. Children with one of these conditions are likely to have dyspraxia too."

DYSPRAXIA

Dyslexia, dyscalculia and dysgraphia can be accompanied by a lack of co-ordination, known as dyspraxia. Children with dyspraxia can have problems with fine motor movement, hand-eye co-ordination and putting things in order, making activities like doing a jigsaw far more challenging than for other children. Dyspraxia can also cause problems with a child's sense of time or direction, and with their memory for lists of events or names.

ADD OR ADHD

Attention deficit disorder or attention deficit hyperactive disorder (ADD or ADHD) causes children problems with concentration. They may find it hard to sit still and be more impulsive than their classmates. Their behaviour can appear much younger than that of children of a similar age and may be disruptive in a school setting.

AUTISM

Autism can cause problems with social interaction: an autistic child may struggle to recognise other people's feelings and express how they feel themselves. Children struggle to understand people's body language and facial expressions, and may have a literal understanding of what you say. They can find it hard to make friends as a result. They lack 'social imagination', the ability to work out how other people will react or make sense of an abstract idea. This can make it hard for them to understand danger or take part in made up games and imaginative play.

Different children have different levels of impairment, so the condition is often called 'autistic spectrum disorder'. Children on the autistic spectrum may have limited speech or have apparently good language yet struggle to understand others. They will enjoy routine, almost to the point of obsession, and need preparation to deal with change. They may be extra-sensitive to light, feelings of touch, sounds, tastes or smells, or may lack sensitivity in some areas. They may have intense interests and obsessive hobbies. Autism can be accompanied by learning disabilities and difficulties in acquiring life skills. Senior Early Intervention teacher Victoria Dawson says, "You might hear the phrase, 'triad of impairment model', which covers the different areas a child may struggle with if they are on the autistic spectrum."

ASPERGER'S SYNDROME

Children with Asperger's syndrome may show similarities to those with autism, but have fewer problems with language and speaking, and may have average or above average intelligence. They can struggle to deal with change, and may therefore respond in an unexpected or unconventional way. They struggle to understand other people's body language, have different ideas about their own and other people's personal space, and as a result have difficulties in social situations. They are likely to be extremely focused on subjects that interest them, which can help if they are interested in a topic at school. Their school work can also benefit from their attention to detail, so their difficulties may not be academic but behavioural.

Suzanne's daughter has Asperger's syndrome. She has managed to work with the school so that both teachers and pupils now understand about Jordan and how her condition affects the way she behaves. Suzanne says, "Bullying began early at school. We helped Jordan by telling her about her disability from an early age, not hiding it from her, and being very open about it. We talked to the school and got them to study Asperger's in more depth. Once the teachers became more educated on the disability themselves things improved. They then went on to establish an anti-bullying scheme."

Suzanne did not need to get a statement of special educational needs for Jordan. She says, "We gave her extra tuition at home to help her keep up. Jordan is now ten and doing brilliantly. As she is nearing high school age, she is still coping with her naivety as her friends grow more mature. If your child is having problems at school, I'd say to go straight to the head teacher and educate them."

MODERATE LEARNING DIFFICULTIES

Some children may not have one specific condition but have general learning difficulties or developmental delay, usually termed 'global developmental delay'. Signs can include poor co-ordination and communication, problems with language and maths, short attention span, and appearing socially immature. Children may have extra difficulties getting organised and understanding where they should be and what they should be doing. They may appear clumsy and find it hard to remember things.

BEHAVIOUR, EMOTIONAL AND SOCIAL DIFFICULTIES

Behavioural, emotional and social difficulties cover a range of conditions, such as depression and eating disorders, and can include attention deficit disorder or attention deficit hyperactivity disorder and syndromes such as Tourette's. Children with these problems can find the way they behave makes it difficult for them to learn, and can cause difficulties, disruption and disturbances for the class. Children can be withdrawn or isolated, hyperactive and lack concentration, have immature social skills or present challenging behaviours. "The first thing to do is look for reasons behind problematic behaviour," explains Tim Francis. "Then, depending on the cause, you can take the most suitable course of action, be it family therapy or rewarding the sort of behaviour you want to encourage."

Diagnosis

If you are concerned that your child may be affected by one of the conditions above, start by talking to your doctor, health visitor, class teacher or SENCO. They can help you work out whether you child is just developing at a different rate to their classmates or whether there might be cause for further investigations.

Express your concerns to the school as soon as possible. This helps your child make the most of their time at school, and avoids them struggling unnecessarily. Older children can find it harder to change their way of learning and behaviour.

A formal identification of any condition can help you understand the sort of difficulties your child is having, and makes it easier for them to get the right sort of help. Victoria Dawson says, "Early intervention is valuable in education. Even if your child is of pre-school age, if you have concerns contact your Health Visitor who can make referrals for further investigation."

PRIVATE SCREENING

If you have the funds and don't want to wait, you could think about a private assessment by a suitably qualified teacher or a Chartered Educational Psychologist specialising in Specific Learning Difficulties. Contact your local Dyslexia Association for a list of professionals. This sort of assessment costs several hundred pounds, for which you get a written report and recommendations about the most appropriate help and support for your child's education.

The report can be taken to the school to help them establish the best ways to work with your child. Occasionally, though, the school will not automatically accept the findings of an independent report. Talk to your local authority Chief Education Officer and ask them to get the school to work with the report. There may also be interventions recommended in the report that the school cannot provide. You will have to go back to the local authority, and possibly through the assessment and statementing processes to get further resources released.

HELP AT SCHOOL

Once you have a diagnosis, or even before, ask the school about how they can help with support and special methods of teaching. Ask how the school will help your child understand their condition and equip them with ways to cope and help them learn.

IDEAS FOR HOW THE SCHOOL CAN HELP

Make sure the school finds out about your child's abilities and strengths. Ask them to build his or her self esteem by using strengths or special interests, and making sure that goals are realistic. Your child needs to experience successes in learning, so targets need to be achievable. In class, can the teacher:

- Provide extra explanations for your child?
- Break a task down into smaller, more manageable steps?
- Check your child understands what they have been told?
- Repeat information in a different way?
- Allow extra time for tasks?
- Tell you what styles of teaching work well for your child?
- Praise your child for their achievements and effort?

Your child can also benefit if there is a regular routine for lessons, so they know what to expect. Can the teacher or assistant help them to remember what they have already learnt about a subject, and go back over points if necessary before moving on? Your child will gain if you and the school can co-ordinate to help them practise key skills. Keep practice sessions short so they stay interested.

Does the school have, or can they acquire, different equipment which might help your child? This is where talking to other parents whose children have similar difficulties can help you find out what is available. Look on the net or ask your local authority about support groups.

OTHER THERAPIES

Talk to your GP about whether your child could be helped by physical, speech, or occupational therapy. The majority of these conditions are for life, but the right help at an early stage can benefit your child enormously.

SPEECH, LANGUAGE AND COMMUNICATION HELP

Your GP can refer your child for speech therapy, although there may be a waiting list. To get the most from an appointment, note down areas where you child has problems and examples of what they say, or can't say. A speech therapist can give you strategies to help your child in areas where they struggle. You may be offered regular help from a speech and language therapist.

Gifted and talented

What if your child is coping well with the work, so well in fact that they complain of being bored? Lack of stimulation can be a cause of bad behaviour. Look at the work your child is doing. You may think that their homework is too simple, and they get all the answers right in minutes. In the first place, talk to the class teacher. They may be setting work to help build your child's confidence, or feel that they need to repeat some lessons to develop an in-depth understanding of the subject.

Duty of schools

Schools have a duty to identify, stretch and challenge bright kids and track their achievement. There should be a lead teacher at every secondary school and at groups of primary schools to help with this. There is a national register for gifted children and a national programme of summer schools for children at secondary level.

How do I know my child is gifted?

According to the Government, your child needs to have 'one or more abilities developed to a level significantly ahead of their year group' to be classed as Gifted and Talented.

What sort of support should my child get?

Ask the class teacher how she or he helps each child to learn at their own rate. Look at the amount of small group work, and whether different groups cover work at different rates or levels. Some schools set up clubs or extra classes. This is not necessarily for 'more of the same' schoolwork, but may set children different sorts of problems to solve, using creative thinking skills.

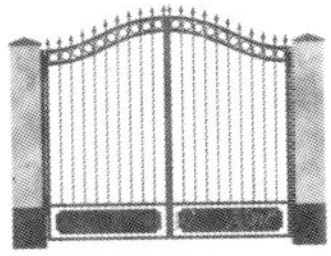

Chapter 2

Social issues and school troubles

In this chapter, read about how to spot that your child may be having problems at school. Find out about causes, how family events can affect children's behaviour, and how best to help your kids. There are lots of tips from families who have been through similar experiences too.

WHAT TO LOOK OUT FOR

Children don't always tell you when they have problems at school. Sometimes you need to watch out for subtle changes. Is your child quieter than usual? Have they stopped talking about school, and no longer want to invite friends home? Do they have headaches, or appear more irritable than usual? Or do they drag their feet more than normal on the way in? Other children act up when they are struggling to deal with something. Educational psychologist Tim Francis says, "Your child is trying to tell you something when they say school is boring, or tell the teacher where to go. Children are herd animals, and don't act outside the herd unless something is wrong."

Reluctance or refusal

Children may appear reluctant to go to school. It can be hard to know whether this is simply a dislike for getting out of bed, or whether there is something more serious at the root. If they often mention a tummy ache or feel sick in the mornings, make an appointment with the GP to rule out health problems. Tim Francis says, "School refusal can be one of the hardest problems to deal with." Parentline Plus offer a 'Troubles at School' leaflet, where they advise, "Seek help as soon as you realise there is a problem ... the sooner the situation is faced the easier it is to deal with."

Time to talk

Take some time to talk about school. Do this in a 'low pressure' way, perhaps while you are doing an activity together or on your way somewhere. Hopefully your child will share any concerns about school. Sometimes refusal to discuss school can indicate that there is a problem which your child is afraid to discuss.

> Laura's son Alexander was very excited about starting school. She says, "He seemed to be socially, emotionally and academically ready to go and so he skipped in the door. Then, he started to have nightmares. We didn't think much of it at first and put it down to his being very tired. He continued to enjoy school. He ran to get there every day and was full of stories about what they'd done when we collected him at home time. And yet, every night before school he had a nightmare."
>
> Alexander's nightmares changed gradually until he was waking drenched in sweat, wild with panic but unable to string together a coherent sentence. Laura says, "Sometimes he didn't recognise us and would frantically try to get away when we went to comfort him. On occasion, he

was not fully awake but was trying to run down the stairs to 'get away'. He would sleep all night once he had calmed down and was unable to remember the incident in the morning. Weekends were a reprieve – he didn't have the night terrors on Fridays or Saturdays."

Laura went into school to speak to the teacher. She says, "I asked if there was anything happening in the class which might be upsetting him but she said that he was the same happy, chatty, chirpy boy we know at home. She assured us that she would keep an eye on him and let us know of any problems". Laura's next move was to read up about nightmares. She says, "I read about 'night terrors' which seemed to fit with what Alexander was going through. They occur most often in the first couple of hours after going to bed. We watched for the pattern and then each night we went to offer him a drink just before he was likely to wake up. The idea of this is to interrupt the sleep cycle. It was pretty tricky because he was not happy about waking up but I just tried to sit him up for a drink and it seemed to break the cycle."

Laura carried on with this strategy and noticed an improvement after three months. She says, "Thankfully, Alexander seems not to be affected by the night terrors. He never mentions them during the day. I had never heard of night terrors but apparently it is quite common, especially when a child faces a new challenge."

Born too late

Some children just are not ready to start school with their peers. Many local authorities now offer part-time nursery places for children from three and reception places after their fourth birthday. If all children start in September, some of those with summer birthdays may find it hard to keep up. If you have concerns about your child's readiness for school, it is still important to fill in school application forms at the same time as everyone else or you may find all the places are filled. Once you have been offered a place, request that your child starts later in the school year, and the local authority should keep their place open for them. Ask for this to be confirmed in writing, and remember that children must start education the term after their fifth birthday. If you are still unsure about school at this stage, you may want to read Chapter 5 which explains about home education.

Handling change

Your child may simply be reluctant to go to school because they are struggling with a change. This could be something expected, like starting a new school or moving up a year, or an unexpected change of teacher or class. Professor Preedy explains, "Every child starts life closely reliant on their parents or carer. It is impossible to avoid life's challenges, but there are ways to help your child mature and handle changes. Be positive, using play and stories to help your child to visualise and experience the positive benefits of change. Do not discuss your child's worries and concerns with others in front of your child."

> Jo's daughter Tiffany found it strange when, on moving into Year 4, she had a male teacher for the first time. Jo says, "She was struggling with the teacher and wouldn't ask for any help. She bottled it all up and became withdrawn and then became angry with close family - mainly me as I'm the person she spends the most time with. She didn't want to tell me anything and didn't like the idea of me going into school. It took a long time to get to the bottom of it."
>
> Jo carried on asking Tiffany about what was upsetting her, and discovered that she found it strange having a man as her teacher. She says, "I told her

that she was not the only one who went through all this and it was a big step for everyone. I told her about my experiences when I was in school and she listened to stories about my school days." Jo then arranged an appointment to see the head teacher and the teacher in question. She comments, "Because Tiffany didn't want me to interfere, I went in without telling her. The school were very good, and they had a word with her but used a softly, softly approach. It was a hard few months to get through but once I went into school and they were aware of the problem she seemed better."

If your child is struggling, Jo advises, "Speak to your child and try and find out the reasons behind it. Go into school and tell them your worries and fears and also talk to other family members or friends." Tiffany is now in Year 6 and happy and confident. Jo says, "She asks more questions in school and has another male teacher this year and she likes him very much."

Learning levels

Find out as much as you can about how your child is getting on with their work. If they are disruptive in class, this can be an indication that they are either struggling with the work or finding they can complete it with ease and still have time to make trouble.

Trouble topics

When talking about school, find out how your child is getting on with their teachers. A statement that they 'hate Mr Smith' is worth investigating further. Have they been in trouble for failing to hand in homework, or disrupting class? Or is there a subject that they are struggling with? You may want to talk to the teacher in question to help your child work things out. If they are reluctant to do that it can be worth talking to the class teacher or head of year instead.

Listening ear

It is important to listen to what your child is saying. If you feel they are only telling you part of the story, ask open questions like, "Tell me more about that ... ?" If they have told you about a problem, ask them what they think might help. Senior Early Intervention Teacher Victoria Dawson says, "Use open questions when you are talking to your child. Say something like, 'Tell me about school', or 'What do you get up to at break time?' Avoid leading questions, where the words in the question can encourage certain answers. A leading question could be, 'Is Mr Smith giving you a hard time?' This doesn't give your child so much scope to explain the problem from their point of view."

Tim Francis recommends listening to your child, then summarising back what you have heard them say. He says, "This helps them know you are listening. Then, keep quiet for a few minutes to see if they will share anything else."

Being me

There are many other things that can leave your child struggling to cope with the day-to-day routine of school As well as academic pressures, teens, and even pre-teens start to feel the pressures of growing up. It can be hard to cope with the physical changes and mood swings, especially if your child is going through these things earlier or later than their peers. Classmates can add to a child's concerns about their body image and relationships too. All this can add up to make your child unhappy at school and reluctant to attend.

Truancy

Older children who travel to school independently have the option of not going in at all if they are having problems, and some children may simply skulk in the cloakrooms to avoid a lesson. Usually they will try to hide this from you, so the first thing you may know about it is when you get a letter or call from the school. If your child is not attending school on an occasional or regular basis, you will face pressure from the school to get them to attend, and the possibility of a fine too. The most important thing is to find what's at the bottom of the problem. It may be that your child is being bullied, feels like they have no friends or can't keep up.

Bullying

If you are worried that your child is being bullied, find some time where you can chat about school without interruption. See if you can find a few minutes when the rest of the family is out, or take them to a café. Ask them who they hang out with at break, or what they do at lunchtime. Your child may be reluctant to tell that they are being bullied. The bullies may have made threats to keep them quiet, so if it comes out, reassure your child that they have done the right thing.

Older children may prefer to talk to a family friend or youth club leader. If you know your child has someone they look up to, why not tell the adult friend you think something might be going on, and ask them to have a chat?

> Connor was eight when his mum, Carolyn, found he was having problems with bullies. She says, "The deputy head was very helpful. He checked out the situation and could see that the trouble started when Connor stood

up for the under-dogs. Fights started when he squared up to any child who was behaving unjustly."

The deputy head talked to Connor and came up with some clear rules. "He told Connor that he didn't have to sort out everyone's problems. He explained that if Connor was being struck by another child, he should warn the child not to hit him again. He then said that he would understand if Connor got hit again after this warning, he might end up hitting back. I was just relieved that the deputy head stood by this promise and ensured that Connor did not get into trouble as long as he stuck to the rules.

Connor felt much better and more in control of this situation as a result. He is now in Year 7. He is a confident child, and is still incensed at unjust behaviour. I still sometimes have to hold him back as he tends to get involved with others' problems."

What is bullying?

Your child may be being hurt, or threatened, either directly or via phone messages or online. Bullying can range from name calling, to damaging your child's gear, to deliberately excluding them from conversations and activities.

Nicola's son, Richard, was subject to persistent bullying both in and out of school. She says, "Problems started when Richard was in primary school. Abuse was shouted at him in the street, even if I was present. We had bricks thrown at our house, children peeing up our gate and his arm was broken by a group of boys."

Nicola approached the school on numerous occasions, but, she says, "The school maintained that Richard was not being bullied and that he was 'playing' me. He has Asperger's syndrome, and the school called me in sometimes because he was having a 'meltdown'. They said that due to his 'difficulties with social communication' that he was 'misinterpreting horseplay', yet even other mothers expressed concern about him being beaten up at playtime."

Nicola found she was hitting a blank with the school, so phoned the local Austism Support Service. They were already involved with Richard, and she was surprised to find that they had made a recommendation that he did not go out at break-time as they had had to physically intervene as he was being beaten. She says, "I was shocked to hear this. Where were the supervisory staff at this point?"

Nicola continues, "At the same time, my younger son Erik was struggling at school, seemed distant and was classed as 'below average'. The school just suggested that we should make an effort to read to him, which was rather insulting as we have a house full of books and read to the boys all the time." Both these events led Nicola to decide school wasn't working for the boys. She decided to take them out of school. She says, "Richard had started to talk about killing himself. After deregistration he had counselling for a couple of years as his mental health had severely suffered whilst at school."

Nicola home-educated the boys for two to three years until Richard chose to try a different school in a different area part-time for a couple of months. This worked well, and he moved to attending full-time a couple of months later.

She says, "He has a Statement of special educational needs. Now he's back in school they tested him and our work at home seems to have helped. He scored very highly on the tests he took at 11, with the age-related achievement level generally placing him at around 16 years."

FACT FINDING

Start by noting down what happened and when so you can fill the school in on the facts. Again, your child may not want to tell the school. Spend some time talking through why they are worried, and how you and the school will be able to work together to help them.

TIME TO TALK

Talk to the teacher. The bullying may be news to the school. Ask about the school anti-bullying policy. Give the details of what has happened and when. Ask clearly what the school plans to do about it, when they will do this, and how they feel their actions will help to stop the bullying.

Arrange for a follow-up meeting and fix up a way to inform the school if the problem recurs. Keep reassuring your child that it is right to tell their teacher every time the bullying happens. The government information website, Direct.gov, has good information about bullying and how to handle it. Also see Chapter 6 for more on homophobic, racist and cyber bullying.

Moving house

A house move can cause children stress, just like adults, especially if it involves a move to a new school. Some children find it harder than others. Try to introduce the idea of the move gradually. Think about what you can do to help your child stay in touch with old friends and make new ones. Arrange play dates for younger kids. See if there is a club or special interest group that your child can join in your new area. This can help children of any age meet new people with the same interests.

Tanya moved house when she was 13. She says, "It had a big effect on my performance and behaviour at school. I'm sure I would have done better in my GCSEs if I had not moved schools then. My behaviour was awful. I was called in to the headmistress's office one morning and I started crying so she left the room to get some tissues and I made a run for it. I just wandered around the town until my mum and her friend caught up with me. I became depressed and resentful towards my parents.

"This went on for a while until the school took note and helped me. They were rubbish at first but after a while there was one lady who took me under her wing, listened to my problems and gave me a chance. I was taken out of mainstream school and had to go to this particular classroom every day. There were some other children there but most days it was just me and her. We played computer games, wrote a lot, and did reading. I went to that classroom for about a year or so before returning to mainstream school which was the hardest thing I ever had to do. That lady, Mrs Bell, was my saviour."

Tanya offers this advice for parents thinking about moving house when their children are teens: "I would say to parents to take into consideration what effect it would have on their children if they move schools. Once you get to secondary school it can be really tough. If your child really hates school and refuses to go, there must be a reason. Please talk to your children and listen to what they have to say and be understanding. If your child can't talk to you about it then let them talk to one of your close family friends. I always found it easier to talk to a family friend than my own parents."

Tanya has left school now, and says, "I did find it very hard to get my first job but got over that. I have very high anxiety and I think this started when we moved."

Kat and family moved house the term after her son started school. Their new home was just a few minutes from their old one, but son Alex found the move tough. Kat says, "Alex has ADHD, which meant the change in routine really affected him. He had a routine for going to school, and knew when we needed to leave and which way we would walk. Alex's behaviour was already difficult and ideally we would have preferred to have moved house during the summer holidays before he started school, but the usual delays in the house-buying process meant this did not happen."

Kat has learnt from her experience, and says, "If you are moving, try to keep your routine as simple and normal as possible. We talked about moving house, and read books about moving house. We told Alex how things would be better when we moved: he would have his own bedroom, and there would be a bigger garden. Alex was worried when we packed his toys that we were taking them away from him forever which must have been a real ordeal for him. We had to explain that the toys were just going in the garage and that he would seem them again really soon. We let him keep his favourite things in a backpack so he felt secure." Kat also suggests that it helps to take your child on visits to the new house. She says, "Let them choose wallpaper, carpets, new bedding and so on. Let them pack their own toys and keep reassuring them that nothing bad is going to happen."

Divorce

Everyone finds divorce traumatic, but it can be extremely confusing for a child who doesn't understand what is going on, and can't control it either. You can help your child by reassuring them that mum and dad both still love them. Work out what you can do to help your child feel secure when established relationships are changing. If you have to move house or change schools, try to establish a new routine with regular contact with both parents.

And when your partner is around, try to avoid direct conflict. There may be things you need to say to each other, but minimise clashes in front of the kids.

Be as honest as you can reasonably be with your children without causing them unnecessary distress. Discourage children from taking sides, and ask family and friends to focus on supporting your children rather than being partisan in front of them. You need to allow your child to talk about your partner – they will be missing their presence even if you are relieved to have them out of the house.

Children will be angry at times, frustrated and find it hard to manage their feelings. They can feel that they are not important to you any more, which can result in emotional turmoil and bad behaviour. See if there is someone outside the family who can offer support for your child. This might be a teacher, a family friend, or your GP may be able to put you in touch with a counsellor. At the same time, look at getting support for yourself so you have someone other than the children to talk to. Try to make space to vent your own hurt and anger. This could be by talking to a friend over coffee, or seeing a professional, or you might want to plan a regular trip to the swimming pool, or time for a long walk.

> Rachel was 13 when her parents divorced. She says, "I was ashamed of what happened. My dad was a teacher at the school and it was a big talking point. I became quite aggressive, started to hang out with undesirable crowds, pushed the boundaries a lot, and started smoking. My marks deteriorated. Inside, I denied anything was wrong – it was the only way I could cope.
>
> "My parents' divorce was particularly vicious: I didn't see my mum for three years. One thing the school did which helped, but perhaps not

intentionally, was to send me on a work placement. It took my mind off things and got me interested in working with children with special needs, which has ended up being my career."

Rachel got divorced herself, when her son was five. She says, "It was a difficult thing to go through for both of us. Ben wet himself at school. He started to get worried whether people were going to pick him up: he felt abandoned. He would cry at anything and hit himself, calling himself a bad boy. It took time to work through this. I spent plenty of time with him, giving cuddles, reassuring him, and talking to him about it. I told Ben's school and they were understanding. Ben didn't open up to them though. They are very discreet, and will make separate appointments for my ex and me at parents' evening without me even having to ask."

Things improved for Ben when Rachel started seeing someone regularly. Rachel says, "I introduced them slowly and gradually Ben got a male role model back in his life and feels more secure. We're both a lot happier. Ben is top of the class. He sees his dad and they have a functional relationship, and there's no more crying or wetting himself." Contact with Rachel's ex is not always easy, though, and she says, "I have to work hard to keep the relationship going between Ben and his dad. I'm not sure how long it will last though. Ben does still want me back with his dad and does get upset about that now and then."

Rachel has learnt a lot from her experiences. "Counselling helped me to move on from my own divorce," she says. "I feel I need counselling about my parents' divorce now as they still score points off each other through me and I hate it."

She has some advice for anyone going through a similar experience: "It's important to be honest with your child, but without being cruel: they don't need to know every last detail. Stick to a routine as much as you can at home, and have an honest dialogue with school about what has happened. Try to keep the child in the same school if at all possible, and both attend school concerts or parents' evening even though you may feel like you can't stand the sight of each other. I found it helpful having a friend going through the same thing and Ben found it useful to know her daughter was experiencing the same.

"Recognise that the child will react in some way, don't be angry about their reaction but just see it as the rollercoaster that they have to travel through in order to come out the other side. Don't focus on all the negatives, look at how well they are coping too and celebrate that, and remember to congratulate yourself too on how well you are doing with the situation. Most importantly, remind your child how much they are loved."

Serious illness

Ongoing health problems can cause children to miss school on a regular basis and make it hard to keep up. Tell the school as soon as you can, and keep them informed about appointments and during periods when your child can't be there. They may be able to arrange for work that your child can do from home. The Special Educational Needs Co-ordinator (SENCO) may have more ideas on how they can help. Talk to the local authority as well. There may be the possibility of a home tutor if absences are regular or prolonged. Your child may also miss out on the social side of school. Plan regular meet-ups as their health allows.

More health issues

It can be just as hard for a child if a family member is seriously ill. They may be angry and resentful as more attention is focused on the sick child, or become quiet and withdrawn in an attempt to be 'good'. The 'well' child may also develop unexpected stomach aches or other psychosomatic illnesses as they feel understandably neglected and see that the person who is ill gets more attention.

Try to make sure that your child has time and opportunity to talk to someone, be it a teacher or friend. Some schools also have counsellors now, or can put you in touch with a local service. Make time to spend with each of your children, even if you feel all your attention should be on the sick child.

Think carefully about how much you involve your child in their sibling's treatment. Hospitals can appear to be scary places, and a visit may help defuse some of their fears. Allow that they may not want to attend every time you visit, and maybe arrange for them to visit a friend some days instead.

> Hannah's sister, Alice, was born severely disabled. Alice's ongoing health problems affected Hannah for much of her time at school. She describes the effects, "I wrote a lot of stories about Alice at primary school. My grandmother took Alice as a foster child, and I was confused why she had gone away. I felt my bad behaviour was to blame, even though I later found out that it was due to my mother having depression.
>
> In the stories I tried to explain what had happened and why Alice had left us." From age 10, Alice's' health deteriorated. When Hannah was 13, Alice was diagnosed with kidney failure. Hannah says, "Things became difficult at home. At school, I didn't think about Alice and didn't talk about her. I was ashamed of having a disabled sister because I had started to notice that people stared at her when we were out. I rarely talked about her to my friends or teachers, even though I felt stressed. Most weekends were spent visiting Alice in hospital, in a ward full of ill children. At school, I wasn't coping. My behaviour wasn't great. I was silly and didn't

concentrate. Several teachers expressed concern. I was told I was in danger of failing my GCSEs and my parents were angry. I started to rebel, wore lots of make-up and dressed provocatively. This got me into trouble and made me unpopular at school."

Things changed dramatically for Hannah when, shortly before her GCSEs, Alice had a successful kidney transplant. Hannah says, "She became 'well' overnight. I felt the pressure disappear: it was like a miracle. I think it is no coincidence that I did much better than expected in my GCSEs. I stopped behaving badly and tried to become the academic my parents said they wanted me to be. Things improved for me at school and I did well. I became more popular, I was the star of the debating society and ended up winning awards. I went to university and got a good degree."

There have been long-term effects for Hannah, who says, "I have suffered with depression and I am sure part of the problem was accumulated stress from my childhood and teens. I had four miscarriages before my son was born. One of the babies I miscarried was severely disabled and this upset me terribly. I had an insight into how my parents must have felt when Alice was born. I have found strength in becoming much closer to my family. They were incredibly supportive during my illness. In a way, I think we were all shocked that I, like Alice, had suddenly become ill."

Hannah has a few things which helped her cope during the difficult times. She says, "In the early years, my grandmother helped me cope. She picked me up from Yorkshire, where I lived, and took me to stay with her. She was kind, spoiling me and helping me sleep by stroking my forehead. During my teens, rebelling gave me a sense of independence. I particularly enjoyed rebelling against my parents' wishes that I visit Alice in hospital every weekend. Now, I feel guilty but it was a natural reaction: I found visiting Alice in hospital disturbing, I was frightened that she would die."

Hannah didn't get any help from the school. In retrospect, she says, 'I don't think I gave the teachers the chance to help, because I had no desire to confide in them. This is a pity, I think, because actually they were kind people and I wish I had talked to them. Even when Alice had her transplant, no one knew about it at school. I had to go in on the day she had the operation and I wish my parents had given me the day off, because I was extremely stressed." Hannah's advice for other families dealing with serious illness: "Talk to each other. Seek therapy or family counselling. Don't assume your children are coping because they won't talk about their stresses. Expect challenging behaviour. Keep your children informed and make sure you inform their school what is going on. If the school doesn't know, it can't help."

Parental illness

If you or your partner is seriously ill, this has its own effects on the child and the whole family. A child may need to help more with siblings, or look after themselves more. In some cases children take on caring for their parent. All these responsibilities can make it hard for the child at school, due to tiredness, or perhaps the thought that, relatively, school does not seem important.

Tell the school what is happening: a quick phone call can make all the difference if your older child ends up late every day as they have to drop their younger brother off. The school can also help with contacts if your child needs someone to talk to. Speak to Social Services to find out about practical help.

Dan, 15, has had a hard time coping with his mum Georgie's illness. Georgie explains, "Dan has taken the brunt of it. He has had to call the ambulance on several occasions. If I pass out he can tell the ambulance driver about what medication I am on and what I am allergic to. It is a source of heartache to me. He shouldn't have to be so capable. He has been my rock when I have been angry or when I'm ill."

The whole family moved more than 100 miles after Georgie became ill, which meant that Dan had to change schools at the age of 12. Georgie says, "He found the move from Essex hard, as he was separated from his friends, and absolutely hated it when he first got there. Nobody knew what was going on with his life and it was difficult for him to have to explain to everyone." Dan comments, "It was all just so much to cope with. I was scared and lonely. It took me time to be able to confide in a teacher."

Georgie continues, "He rebelled, smoked cannabis and drank. Basically, he got in with the wrong crowd. The school were supportive, particularly the head of year. We had to get him some counselling to help him talk through all the stuff he's been through. He used to come back saying, 'All we did was talk,' but it seems to have helped. The community police took notice too. Our local officer discovered that he was interested in joining the police and she has been around to help him keep on the straight and narrow. He still has a lot of anger inside him, which can burst out unexpectedly: the other week he punched a wall after a blow-up with a friend. He and I are very open and can talk about things, though. He has a good network of friends in and out of school, and they all come in and out of our house."

Death

If a family member or friend dies, you child may seem to take it all in their stride, but their worries can appear in different ways. Children can also be affected strongly by the death of a pet.

Younger children have little understanding of death, just as they may be unclear about the difference between today and tomorrow. They may think that the person will return. A primary school age child will be frightened by death, and probably aware that it is final. By eight or nine your child will have a clearer understanding of death, depending on their maturity and experiences. Teenagers' reactions may be more extreme as they are going through a period of strong feelings and emotions.

> Fiona's children were nine, seven and four when their dad died suddenly. She says, "All of them lost confidence. The older two also found it very hard to concentrate for several months and their work suffered. Teachers were mostly sympathetic and understanding." Fiona's youngest child coped best, but became clingy at dropping-off time.
>
> Fiona says, "The one thing that really upset me was when the whole class made Father's Day cards. His teacher confused him completely by explaining that as I now did all his dad's chores at home, I was like his dad as well as his mum, so he could do a card for me. This upset me too because it seemed to negate his dad. My children have the best dad in the world, who just doesn't happen to be alive any more. I'm not their dad. I just couldn't understand why they had to make the cards at all. Every parent in the class knew about my husband's death and they would all have understood completely if they hadn't made cards."
>
> Fiona's eldest child's behaviour became disruptive at times: he had had intermittent behaviour problems due to Asperger's traits in the past. Fiona says, "The school didn't cope with this and responded with sticks instead of carrots, which just made his behaviour far worse. After much fruitless discussion with his head teacher I felt I had no option but to take him out of the school. This solved the problem instantly."
>
> Problems do not always show up straight away. Fiona's middle child appeared to be happy, but more than a year later started complaining of feeling sick, especially on school days. She says, "The school were again supportive and, after we ruled out other options, recognised that this was

a long-term reaction to his dad's death. He hated being away from home, I suppose in case anything happened to me unexpectedly too. The school allowed him to stay off games for a few weeks as he felt sick, and arranged some bereavement counselling for him."

Fiona concludes, "Their dad's death affected all three children very differently, and the school's ability to cope varied too. I think the loss of confidence and poor concentration would affect the majority of children in this situation, but other reactions can vary considerably and go on for months and even years."

Listening and feeling

Listen to your child and try to understand what they are thinking. Like adults, children can feel loss and grief, shock, anger and guilt after someone has died. Children will grieve, but may do so in short spurts, then appear to get on with their everyday activities. Others can put off grieving until they are emotionally ready.

Denial, guilt, anger and fear

The classic reactions after a death are denial, guilt, anger and fear, and these feelings can occur in different orders, or even all together. Your child may carry on talking about someone as if they are still alive, which can be distressing for you and other relatives. This is just part of denying that the death has happened. Children often feel guilty and wonder if they are to blame for a death.

They may feel angry towards the dead person for not being there, or towards a surviving parent, or towards their friends who have not had a similar loss. They will also worry about being different from their peers, which may make it hard to talk about how they feel when they are at school. Children may seem to go back a few stages, or become more clingy out of fear that they will lose other loved ones.

> When Caroline was 18 one of her mum's younger sisters died of cancer. She says, "My aunt's death completely devastated me. It made me realise that school was really a very small part of the life cycle and after she died, learning didn't seem that important for a while and I failed all my A Levels. I think my parents expected me to get over it, but as she was one of my favourite aunts, it didn't seem possible. To add to the death, at the same time, I had been ill, and I had one teacher who seemed hell-bent on persecuting me. It all meant that I found being in the sixth form very difficult. It didn't exactly help either that I also seemed to have my finger permanently on the self-destruct button."
>
> Although Caroline had problems at school, she also found help there. "I had one teacher who literally saved me from myself. With hindsight, I think I was so angry and didn't really have anywhere I could put it. I was technically an adult but I'd never had anyone in the family die that I was close to. On top, no one prepared me for that moment when the phone call came – it totally throws you."
>
> Caroline suggests that if your teenager is struggling with a loss, "try and give them time and space to sort themselves out; everyone deals with loss and grief differently and there's no 'right' or 'wrong' way to do it. You just end up grieving – and then one day it just seems to stop hurting quite so much."

Helping your child

It can be very hard to help your child through grief when you have lost someone too. The things to remember are to talk to your child, to be clear and honest about the death, and to listen to them. Reassure them that there is no blame attached to them, the death is not their fault in any way, and that it is OK to have all sorts of feelings. Show them you accept their feelings, and share how you feel too. Work out how you can remember and commemorate together the person who has died. Children may want to be allowed to say goodbye, or I love you, or I miss you, or whatever else they feel they missed saying while the person was alive.

Day to day, try to provide your child with reassurance that life can go on as normal, as far as possible. Stick with usual routines as far as is practically possible. Some children may need a physical outlet for all their feelings, so build in time for activities such as riding a bike, swimming, kicking a ball around together, or going for a walk. Professor Preedy has some more suggestions: "Stories can help your child to grieve and understand their feelings. Through the story you can remember the good times and start to come to terms with the loss. Supporting your child when they lose a pet can also be an opportunity to prepare for the loss of a loved one."

Rose's father died after a short and unexpected illness at the end of the summer term. Her son, Karl, was seven at the time. Rose says, "He had a fantastic infant school teacher who completely understood what we were going through as a family. It was dreadful that I was not there to collect him from school on the last day of infants as it was quite a special leaving day." Karl then moved up to his junior school, but was unsettled.

Rose says, "He had been so close to his grandfather that the death was unthinkable. He really needed someone to understand what he was going through. The school didn't seem to make any allowances and any misdemeanour of Karl's was pounced on heavily."

Rose eventually got help for her son outside the school. "We found a brilliant group called Chums who ran four-week coping with bereavement sessions for children and adults, and that was the best thing ever. It really helped my son. I just saw a poster for it one day at the doctor's and self referred."

Karl is now 10 and has settled at school, having come to terms with his grandad's death. Rose comments, "He says that he does not think about it every day now but can think about grandad in a nice way."

From her experiences, Rose has some tips to help other families. She says, "Use the internet or read for an understanding of how a child experiences death. It can be quite different to an adult's grief. Show your feelings in front of your children. It's no use saying 'you have to be strong for the kids'. It hurts and they need to know that it is all right to cry and that you don't get over people in five minutes. Remember the deceased. On my father's birthday we have a cake and let the wind blow out the candles. His memory is very much alive all the time and my son can ask anything about what happened. We celebrate days that were special to him: we love St Patrick's and Halloween because they were important to my father."

Grief and school

It can be difficult to decide when your bereaved child should go to school. There is a balance to be struck between letting life go back to some sort of normal, and allowing your child the time and space they need. Professor Preedy says, "Going to school gives a child the chance to be a child, whereas at home they may be taking on more responsibility, especially if a parent has died." Some children may be reluctant to go to school at all, perhaps being afraid that something might happen while they are away from their family. You need to decide what is a reasonable period away from school, and when, in fact, they might be better off getting on with their usual activities. Again, listen to what your child is saying, reassure them, and talk to the school about how they are feeling.

At school children may find it hard to concentrate on the work in hand. Tell the school what has happened so they can understand if your child's behaviour changes. Sometime children can take their anger at a death out on their peers. They may start bullying, telling lies or being aggressive. This can be difficult to handle, especially if you are not feeling 100 percent yourself. Ask the teacher to talk things out with your child, as they may benefit from sharing feelings with someone outside the situation.

Sometimes it can take some help from the school to move a situation on. Professor Preedy explains, "A seven year old girl always seemed sad in class and had difficulties with friendships. She built up a close relationship with a nursery nurse, who found out that her baby sister had died some time ago. There were still lots of reminders of the baby at home but the child had not been to the funeral. She told the nursery nurse one day that she 'hadn't said goodbye' to her baby sister. With the nursery nurse's help she wrote a letter which she and her parents took to the cemetery. This enabled the parents to understand how their daughter felt and helped them all to move forward."

MORE SUPPORT

This book can only touch on some of the issues that can cause problems for your child. If you know that they are going through a traumatic life event or experience, tell the school. Ask for help, for yourself and your child. Tim Francis comments, "Talk to your child's head of year or SENCO. They may know of a local bereavement centre, or how to get some written materials or access to a counsellor. Use the referral system." You can also call the local authority children's services department, or talk to your GP if you are unsure where to start. Look on the internet or in your local library for details of help groups, as you don't have to struggle alone.

Chapter 3

Work it out with the school

This chapter looks at how to start solving problems at school. Read on to find out about your rights and how to complain. You will also find stories about how other parents have liaised with schools to find solutions.

MAKING THE PROBLEMS KNOWN

You may be worried that talking to the school may make the problem worse. Indeed, your child may ask you not to tell the teachers what is going on. In general, schools want to know what is happening and most problems are easier to solve if you are working with the school. Often, the teacher is not aware of the problem, which can make it hard to find a resolution.

What have other parents raised?

Parents bring many matters to a school's attention. A good school will want to address problems, and speaking up about a problem that your child is experiencing can help other kids. You can talk to the school about:

- The subjects your child is studying, or would like to study
- Faith and religious education at school
- Sex education
- The quality of teaching and teaching methods in general
- The standards and methods of a particular teacher
- Personality clashes between a member of staff and your child
- Too much or too little homework
- Your child's results and the way their work is marked
- Clashes with classmates, making friends, and bullying
- School resources
- Treatment of children with special needs
- How the school disciplines children

You have a right to complain to your child's school, and the school must have a procedure in place to deal with your complaints. In the first place you may be able to resolve matters with an informal chat. Professor Preedy says, "Most schools make it easy to contact the teacher. A lot of issues, like falling out with a friend, can and should be dealt with as soon as possible. We make it possible for parents to email the teacher, which can make it easier for busy working parents to quickly and easily sort out any issues."

Rachel has sorted out a problem swiftly by talking to the class teacher informally. She says, "Ben was put next to a new girl who was swearing at him. I wanted to sort this out quickly, so nipped in after school. I had got my concerns clear in my mind and worked out how I wanted them resolving. Ben needs to sit in this particular spot due to his visual problems. I was very smiley and positive and stated my concerns. I asked for the new girl to be moved. The teacher didn't confirm she would do this, but it did happen."

INFORMAL COMPLAINTS

Who should I talk to?

Contact the school and arrange to talk to your child's class teacher, or possibly a senior teacher like the head of year. You probably want to choose someone who has direct contact with your child and is in a position to help with the situation. If your child has special needs you may want to talk to the SENCO. Bear in mind that they may not be aware of the issue. Explain why you are coming, to give the teacher a chance to assess the situation and think about it in advance of your meeting.

Professor Preedy advises, "Don't be too quick to assign blame. Explain the issue to the teacher and see what their take on the matter is. Often the teacher will need to investigate the situation and get back to you. Be prepared that your child may not have told you the whole story. We had a parent complain that their child was coming home saying they never got anything to eat and the food was terrible. A teacher observed the child for a few days, and found that they always ate a decent meal, so we needed to look for other reasons why the child was trying to get attention by complaining."

> Helen's daughter was unhappy at school, but Helen found it hard to approach the school in the first place as, she says, "Nothing was being done directly to our daughter, it was the general atmosphere of the school. There was awful language, children threw food over each other at lunchtime, the toilets were difficult to use as people were smoking and hanging about in there."
>
> The family supported daughter Emily as much as possible, and when she started losing weight and becoming anxious, Helen decided she had to

take the issue to the school. She explains what she did. "I put a request in writing to meet the head of year. I also sent a statement of issues that I would be raising. When we met, the year head did listen and take on board my strong concerns. He suggested a number of ideas. We tried some of his suggestions, but that brought about further problems as Emily became more noticeable by not eating in the lunch hall, and using the staff loo. It did not solve anything.

"The real problem of the loud unruly behaviour by some was 'beyond the year head's control,' in his own words. He explained at length the great difficulty in removing such students from school, it was almost impossible and, whilst he understood, little more could be offered. At that point we decided to throw our energy into supporting and teaching Emily fully at home, rather than trying to change a system."

When to meet

It may be easiest to have a meeting without your child being there, or you may feel strongly that they need to attend. If you can meet the relevant teacher in school hours it can be easy to do so without your child. If the teacher is only available after school, say, you may want to ask a friend to take your child after school so you can discuss the issue.

Mum Michaela has four children at different stages in their school career, so has had to meet the school on various occasions. She says, "If it is something serious I don't make an appointment. I go in and if they're not available I wait. I always feel it gives me an edge. I don't accept platitudes and always come away with a verbal agreement as to the action that is going to be taken. I make a point of reiterating the points agreed, and give a timescale that is acceptable for the required action. If I have more than one point I write a note and refer to it."

What to say

It can help if you prepare yourself in advance of a meeting. Make rough notes of what you want to talk about. You might want to write down times and dates of specific incidents. If you want to talk about academic work you may want to ask the teacher to have your child's schoolbooks at the meeting.

> Mother of three and former school governor Belinda shares her tips for getting the most out of a meeting with the school:
>
> - Write a basic list of the topics you want to cover.
> - Take a pen and notebook into the meeting with you and make notes.
> - Do not lose your rag, it will help nobody.
> - Summarise the meeting clearly using your notes.
> - Get the head to agree an action plan.
> - Follow it up in writing.
> - If necessary copy in the Chair of the Governors and the local authority.

How to say it

Think about how you feel before you go into the meeting. If you are angry and upset, it can help to admit this out loud. Explain how you feel to the teacher, but try to do so calmly so that you can productively work together with the school to address the issue. Be prepared to listen to any responses and to accept that there are always two sides to any story. Professor Preedy says, "Preparation on both sides is important." If you are worried that the teacher won't listen to you or understand, you could practise explaining the problem to a friend. You may want to bring your partner or a friend to the meeting for support. It can help to let the school know who will be attending.

Jane met with her son's school on a number of occasions to try to stop bullying. She says, "It all started after we'd moved. My son, then aged 12, started at a new school and was bullied, physically and mentally, almost from day one." Jane brought the issue to the attention of the school on numerous occasions. She says, "As we didn't know his class teacher that well we first went to the head of year. She tried to sound surprised when we explained the issue. I spoke to her numerous times, and was frustrated that she still tried to express surprise and was unaware that the bullying had continued and worsened.

"I lost count how many times we met. We then met the deputy head and finally the head teacher, although it was a battle to get an appointment with him. I had telephoned on numerous occasions too. They seemed totally unaware of the severity of the damage being done. Steven had stopped learning, his work had deteriorated to such a level that there really was no point in him being at the school."

What action can a school take?

You may be quite clear about how you would like a problem to be addressed. It will help if you can have some ideas of what would improve things for your child. Listen to what the teacher suggests too. In the first place, it may be helpful if the teacher listens to your child and hears what they have to say about the problem. The teacher can then reassure the child that his problem is being taken seriously and talk through possible changes.

Professor Preedy says, "Use the support that the school offers. Talk to other parents, see if the parents' association can help too. Don't be isolated in dealing with your problems."

It might be right for the teacher to talk to another child, or group of children, if they are causing the problem. Alternatively, the teacher may feel it is better to talk to the whole class.

Laura's daughter Aaliyah was unhappy when some girls who were previously good friends starting leaving her out. Laura says, "It wasn't until she lied and said that one of them said that her father would kill her that the teachers finally took it seriously. She sat the whole class down and talked to them about being nice to each other." Laura continues, "The school was understanding, and this helped, but in the end they can't make children be friends with each other. Much as you would like to sort out your child's entire universe, sometimes they have to grow up and learn not to rely too much on particular friends.

"My daughter now has a new, wider set of friends. She values their kindness and moves on if they are being silly."

Other ways to help

The teacher may change their behaviour, giving your child extra praise if they need to build confidence. The teacher may take time to pay more attention to the child's interactions with others if they are being bullied. It can be helpful to ask the teacher to involve the staff who supervise the children at break time and dinner time.

Denise and her son Deacon, five, were reading a story together when Deacon said, "I don't want to go to school tomorrow as some boys have been kicking me." Denise saw the bruises and welts and reassured Deacon that she would sort it out. She says, "The teacher is very approachable. I just went in first thing and spoke to her in the classroom. She got down to Deacon's level and asked who had kicked him. She reassured him too, and told him he could tell a dinner supervisor if it happened again. She then promised to sort things out during the day."

The boys were in reception, the year below Deacon. There was an assem-

> bly for the infants that day, and the teacher took action, asking anyone who had been kicking in the playground to own up. She then explained that they shouldn't do this, which seems to have nipped the problem in the bud."

Rearrangements

It may be that your child's problems can be solved by simple rearrangements. Would they find it easier to hear what the teacher is saying if they were moved closer to where she teaches from? Or if your child struggles to get everything done in time, is there a way to allow them extra time for tasks?

> At school Matt was constantly frustrated; his greatest difficulty was copying from the board. Mum Liz says, "It takes him much longer than other students as he is dyslexic. We spoke to the class teacher who assured us that the homework was written on the board at the start of the lesson. However, in reality this was not always the case. The result was Matt would be kept behind and arrive flustered at the next lesson, probably reprimanded for being late and in no fit state to learn."

Beating bullying

The school should have an anti-bullying policy. Ask what this involves. How will the teachers assess the situation, how will they talk to the bully?

It can be hard to change other children's behaviour. There are anti-bullying organisations and resources which can help you make suggestions about how the school can act to change things. Check out:

- The Department for Children, Families and Schools website on bullying, **www.dfes.gov.uk/bullying** which includes guidance on cyber-bullying.
- The Anti-bullying Alliance website, **www.anti-bullyingalliance.org.uk** has lots of resources and ideas for schools including:
  - Anti-bullying assemblies
  - Anti-bullying audit toolkit
  - Anti-bullying charter for schools
  - A list of books for children about bullying
  - A briefing on making schools safer
- The NSPCC has a series of guidance booklets called Checkpoints, with versions for Schools, Young People (aimed at Year 6 preparing for secondary school or Year 7) and for parents. You can send off for these or download them from **www.nspcc.org.uk**.

Alongside action at school you can help to build your child's confidence and help them develop friendships by inviting classmates home and encouraging involvement in school activities.

> Nell was shocked to find her daughter being bullied in her first year at school. She says, "Dee was four at the time. Her friend Shana had her fifth birthday in January, which seemed to be a catalyst. Shana decided that since she was five, Dee should do what she said. Dee wasn't equipped to deal with this. She was clear that she didn't want to argue with her friend or be rude to her, but neither did she want to be told what to do every playtime. She came home from school every day complaining how Shana had been unpleasant to her.
>
> "I tried to help Dee sort it out for herself, but without success, so I made

an appointment with the teacher. We met after school and I explained the problem. The teacher was keen to sort this out, and agreed to pay more attention to how the girls were interacting. She discussed what could be done with the Head of Early Years, and came up with a strategy, which focused on changing Shana's behaviour.

"Dee was told to tell the teacher or assistant if anything happened, and I checked with her after school how her day had been. It all seemed to die down after a while, Shana was told that she couldn't expect other children to do what she told them, the teachers kept an eye on them as far as they could and, of course, Dee had her fifth birthday too."

Carrots and sticks

Some children may need to change their own behaviour. You can use incentives to help encourage children to stick at work they find challenging, to attend school regularly and on time, or to address anti-social behaviour and discipline problems.

Work out a clear target for your child to aim for with the class teacher, and possibly the head or head of year too. Break this down into smaller parts if necessary, so that your child can experience success. Work out what will encourage your child to stick at it. For younger children this can be simply ticks on a chart leading to a sticker at the end of the day. Older children may be motivated by the offer of a much-wanted DVD or trip to the cinema. The school may have incentive and behaviour schemes of their own, which you should be told about.

Kate, a secondary teacher, says, "We try to focus on the good rather than the bad and send postcards and letters home to parents when a child behaves well. We also reward with merits. Those with 50 or more merits at the end of the half term get to go on a free school trip, bowling or whatever. It isn't too hard to get the merits you need for the trip."

Kate has used a similar idea for her own daughter. She says, "My six year old was sulky at school and kept having tantrums. I came up with an idea to encourage good behaviour. Charlie takes a little note pad to school for her teacher to write a note and place a sticker in if she behaves well during the day. If she gets a sticker for every day she chooses a magazine at the weekend.

"Obviously this needs input from home and school, but, in the two weeks we have used the book so far, she has made such a big turnaround that TAs and dinner ladies were stopping her teacher in the corridors to say how they couldn't believe how well she was doing and it was like having a different child. She has been given a 'gold book' award which was a certificate for 'improvement in attitudes towards learning' and has just been so much better generally."

Whatever behaviour change you are trying to achieve, it is important that everyone is clear and consistent. Each teacher needs to be aware of what is expected and what the rewards are. You need to back up the school, and encourage your child too.

MORE HELP

If you're struggling to change your child's behaviour look at this checklist

- What is causing the problem – is there anything that should be changed to help your child?
- Is your child clear how you expect them to behave? Make up achievable targets for them.

- Are all your child's teachers clear about your child's targets for behaviour?
- Is your child praised consistently for good behaviour? Devise a strategy to reward their efforts with something that will motivate them.

Putting things in context

With 30 years of experience as a teacher, and 20-plus years as a parent, Professor Preedy has a few words to help you put your child's problems in context. She says, "Things aren't going to be fine all the time. Life often isn't fair; children will get on better with some teachers than others, but you want to look at the overall package. I wasn't happy at all with one of my daughter's teachers. He didn't seem up to the mark when it came to written work and marking. However, he had a wonderful general and subject knowledge and talked to the students a lot. In retrospect, I think she got a lot from him emotionally and educationally: I hadn't appreciated that at the time."

A FORMAL COMPLAINT

Going to the head

You may decide to talk to the head teacher. You could do this in the first place, if you feel that they have more control over the relevant situation, or you may choose to go to them if you have not got a resolution with the class teacher or head of year. If you're not sure how to arrange to see the head, talk to the school receptionist or secretary. Some heads make a regular time each week to be available to parents too.

Put it in writing

If a meeting with a teacher does not lead to a plan to sort the problem that you are happy with, you may want to become more official and put a complaint in writing. Be as clear as you can. It helps if you can note down significant incidents, and the dates that they happened, as well as who was involved. Think about the outcomes you are seeking. What would you like to see happen? You can write this in the letter so the school is clear about what you want to achieve. You probably want to address the letter to the head at this point. Check out your school's complaints procedure, as they may have appointed someone else as first point of contact for complaints.

Complaints procedure

Ask your school for a copy of their complaints procedure: the advice in this book is general, and your own school's complaints procedure may be slightly different. The complaints procedure should tell you when to expect a letter simply stating they have got your complaint, and when to expect a full written response. There may be information on the school website and there should be some help about how to complain on your local authority website too. The school should respond according to their policy, within a certain period of time. Complaints should be addressed as soon as reasonably possible. Putting a complaint in writing may focus the head's attention on the issue and achieve the change that you want. If not, you can bring in outside help.

Complaining to Governors

If you have had no satisfaction from talking to the class teacher and head teacher, the next stage is to contact the chair of the school Governors, or Parent Council in Scotland. The governing body should have an official complaints procedure. Ask the school for a copy of the procedure so you know what to do. Ask about the timescale for looking into your complaint, so you know what will happen and when. Ideally your complaint should be acknowledged within seven school days. You should get a full response within around 20 school days. This may vary according to an individual school's complaints policy.

What do Governors do?

In England, Northern Ireland and Wales, Governors help run a school by setting its direction. In Scotland, Parent Council members fulfil a similar function to Governors, although as each school can write the constitution for their own parent council, exact responsibilities can vary. A school is run on a day-to-day basis by the head teacher. Governors do not have responsibility as individuals, but the governing body has legal duties and powers.

How can they help me and my child?

Governors can have input to school procedures and policy, including disciplinary matters and target setting. Similarly in Scotland, Parent Council members can have input into school policies discipline, dress, sport, bullying and homework.

Can a Governor back you in a disagreement with the school?

While it can be helpful to get a Governor 'on your side', they do not have the power on their own to make a school change a policy, or a teacher change behaviour. The Governors will discuss this sort of issue and will probably hold a vote to decide a verdict.

By all means tell a Governor about your situation. They may offer a useful perspective or have experience of how the school has solved similar problems for other children.

Can Governors make the school change?

If the Governors feel strongly about a matter of policy they can discuss it at a meeting. They may propose an idea, hold a vote and come up with a way for the school to change. The head teacher is then responsible to the Governors for actually implementing the change.

If the Governors do not deal with your complaint to your satisfaction, you can then write to the clerk of Governors requesting that your complaint be heard by a complaints committee of Governors. This is a meeting of Governors drawn from the governing body, who will meet within around two to four weeks of receiving your letter. You should hear their verdict within five days of their meeting.

If you believe your complaint was not handled fairly according to a school's complaints procedure, you can ask your local authority to investigate, but only after you have been through the school's procedures. Write and explain your complaint. Explain how the school did not follow its complaints procedure, with as much detail as you can. A complaints officer will look at your evidence and decide if it should be investigated. You will get a letter within two weeks telling you what will happen next. The officer only investigates whether the school followed procedure, and does not look at the content of your complaint. If procedure has been followed, they can't make a school change its verdict on a case.

The complaints officer will tell you the outcome of the investigation in writing. If they decide that the school did not follow its procedures, the matter will be referred back to the chair of the governing body. The governing body should then re-investigate the complaint.

EDUCATIONAL EXPERTS

If you feel your child is struggling with work, or their needs are not being met, you may want to get in touch with the local authority education welfare officer or educational psychologist. They can provide an independent opinion, may offer suggestions how to deal with a problem, and may talk to the school on your behalf.

> Jane had a number of meetings at her son's school to try to stop bullying. When meeting the head of year and the deputy head had no effect, she went to the local authority. She says, "I spoke to the local authority, but the responses were at best patronising: they seemed put out because I contacted the head person at their department instead of going through all the different levels. I spoke to the Educational Welfare Officer, who agreed to attend a meeting with the head of the school, but she only offered limited support as an observer."

If you are not satisfied with the way your complaint has been handled by the local authority, you can appeal to the Secretary of State for the Department for Education in your country or your Local Government Ombudsman. There are contact details at the end of this chapter. Ask for a copy of their complaints procedure, which in some cases is available on their websites.

Going further

If you believe that your school or local authority has behaved unreasonably or not fulfilled their duties, you have the right to go to the Secretary of State in the Department for Children, Schools and Families in England, the Education Department for Scotland, Wales or Northern Ireland as appropriate. You can only involve the department once the school and the local authority have finished looking into the complaint.

An Ombudsman can investigate problems in the way the local authority looked into your complaint. This covers issues like not giving you the right information, not dealing with your complaint, or taking too long to do so. The Local Government Ombudsman does not look at how schools and colleges are run.

USEFUL RESOURCES AND CONTACTS

If your child has special educational needs you can go to an SEN Tribunal. Read more about this at **www.sentribunal.gov.uk**

England

Local Government Ombudsman
The Commission for Local Administration in England
Millbank Tower
Millbank
London SW1P 4QP
www.lgo.org.uk

Secretary of State for Children, Schools and Families
Sanctuary Buildings
Great Smith Street
London SW1P 3BT

Northern Ireland

Department of Education for Northern Ireland

Rathgael House
Balloo Road
Bangor BT19 7PR
www.deni.gov.uk/

The Ombudsman
Freepost
Belfast BT1 6HN

The Ombudsman's Office
33 Wellington Place
Belfast BT1 6HN

Scotland

The Education Department for Scotland
The Scottish Government
Victoria Quay
Edinburgh EH6 6QQ
0131 556 8400

The Scottish Public Services Ombudsman
4 Melville Street
Edinburgh EH3 7NS
0870 011 5378
www.spso.org.uk/

Wales

The Department for Children, Education, Lifelong Learning and Skills has offices throughout Wales. Call 0845 010 3300 for your local contact

http://new.wales.gov.uk

Public Services Ombudsman for Wales

1 Ffordd yr Hen Gae

Pencoed CF35 5LJ

01656 641 150

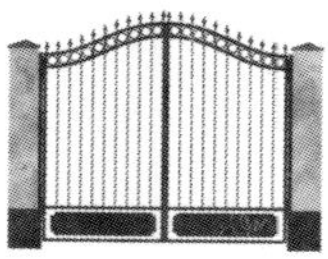

Chapter 4

Changing schools

You may be at the point where your efforts to work things out with the school seem to make no difference. No parent likes to see their child struggling, whether it is because the school can't meet their needs or because of problems like bullying. If you want to find out your options for changing school and other parents' experiences of moving schools, read on.

CHOOSING ANOTHER MAINSTREAM STATE SCHOOL

If you want to move your child to another mainstream state school, you need to start by approaching your local Children's Services or Education Department at the local authority. You may already have a school in mind, and they can tell you if it has a vacancy. The authority will have a list of schools in your area with available places.

FINDING SCHOOLS

There are online databases in the UK you can search to find local schools.

- England: Schoolfinder **http://schoolsfinder.direct.gov.uk/**
- Scotland: Parentzone **www.parentzonescotland.gov.uk/ChoosingASchool/SearchForASchool.asp**
- Wales: Schools in Wales **www.ngfl-cymru.org.uk/6-0-0-0_schools_in_wales.htm**
- Northern Ireland: Department for Education **www.deni.gov.uk/ http://www.denidata.nics.gov.uk/appinstitutes/instmain.aspx**

You may not want to send your child to one of the local state schools with available places, or there may not be a place available. Go on to page 87 to read about independent schools, or Chapter 5 to read about home education, tutors and flexi-schooling.

What does your child want?

Ask your child what they would like in their new school. Friends can be all-important and going to a school where they know someone already may make settling far easier. If your child has a keen interest in music, sport, art or drama, provision of the right facilities or interested staff could be key to their enjoyment. Listen to your child, and note down a few of their priorities to help you sift through possible schools.

Look at your local schools

Before you go further, it is advisable to visit the schools which have places. Contact the school directly. Some may offer regular tours at certain times each week or month, while others will arrange a tour to suit you. It can be a chance to see the head teacher, pick up a prospectus and possibly meet some of the pupils. You can check out the school's specialist subject areas or facilities for music, sports or computer studies.

What to ask when you visit

Make a list of things to check out when you visit. You might want to ask about:

- the dress code and uniforms
- healthy eating
- arrangements for lunch and break times
- playground activities
- after school activities
- support if your child has special needs
- anti-bullying and behaviour policies
- whether classes are mixed ability or in sets
- homework
- whether there is a school council or parent association
- staff turnover
- how the school keeps in touch with parents
- where leavers go – which secondary schools or colleges

Look at school facilities. Are they well maintained? Does the library look as though it is well used? Check out the provision of computers, and whether they are used in class or just in a single computer room. Other indicators of a well-functioning school can be seen on the walls. Read the notices to see what activities are going on. Look out for well-maintained and up-to-date displays of work, or reports back from school trips. Look into as many classrooms as possible to get an idea of how well the children settle to work.

Carole Anne moved both of her children from one primary school to another. She says,

"My younger son was approaching Year 3 and my elder one was approaching Year 5. They had been attending a large primary, and my husband had been the Chair of the PTFA. Our younger son, however, became the target for a child who had been taken into the school on a scheme to re-integrate children who had previously been excluded. After my son's coat had been cut twice in one week, I complained to the headmaster. He explained that this other child was 'worth' three times the funding that my child attracted."

Carole felt that the head's attitude meant that her son could continue to be targeted, so she started to look for other options. She says, "I visited a lovely little Church of England junior school and arranged to transfer the boys in September. Alan grew six centimetres and went from being described as 'average' to being top of his class by the first Christmas, but Phil struggled to adapt a bit more. He, nevertheless, left at the end of Year 6 with a school prize for sporting achievement and with Level 5 SAT results, above the expected performance for his age group."

School performance

Each year, schools get a performance assessment. Sometimes known as league tables, the school receives a score for the achievements of their pupils. As well as the academic successes, you also want to look at the CVA, or Contextual Value Added score: simply, how much the school has helped pupils improve. This takes into account the fact that some schools are in more deprived areas, have a greater number of children with English as a second language or special educational needs, and other factors that can affect the school's outcomes. Ask the school for their results.

School inspection reports

Your local authority should offer information about all their schools. It can tell you facts such as the number of places available, the number of applications, whether a school is selective, and its success rates for exams. As well as visiting the school and reading the local authority information and school prospectus, you may want to read about the results of the most recent independent inspection. The inspectors write a report which outlines what a school does well, areas of improvement since the last inspection, and where it needs to make further improvements. The school may have copies of their report available for you to read. You can also view reports on the website for the inspection organisation for your area:

- In England the inspections are carried out by the Office for Standards in Education, Children's Services and Skills. You can download inspection reports from **www.ofsted.gov.uk**. State schools in England are inspected every three years.
- In Scotland the inspections are carried out by HM Inspectorate of Education. You can download reports from **www.hmie.gov.uk**. Schools in Scotland should be inspected at least once while a child is there, so every six or seven years. This can be an initial inspection or a follow up. Visit **www.scottishschoolsonline.gov.uk** to search for information by school.

- In Wales the inspections are carried out by Estyn. Each school is inspected every six years. You can download reports from **www.estyn.gov.uk**.
- In Northern Ireland the inspections are carried out by the Education and Training Inspectorate, **www.etini.gov.uk**. Each school is inspected every seven years. You can download reports from **www.denidata.nics.gov.uk**.

Does it feel right?

It can be incredibly hard to make a decision about your child's education based on a single visit. Before making a decision, you may want to make an extra appointment to discuss your child's needs with the head, to see if the school can meet them. If you know someone who has kids at the school already, ask them about what they feel the school does well, and where it falls short. The more people you can ask, the better you can see if there are any general problems with the school. Remember that reputations build up over years and may not reflect current practice at a school. Talk to the kids as well as the parents for interesting insights on areas where the school excels.

> Peter was bullied off and on for several years. Parents Denise and Mike had been in to the school on numerous occasions before they decided to move both their sons to another school. Denise says, "It started with some name calling. We had met informally with the teacher, and probably had around 10 more formal meetings over a couple of years. I also asked his class teachers how he was getting on every week – but there were several changes of teacher which didn't help. It was a small school, with only 14 kids in Peter's class, so it was hard for him to make different friends.

"We were unhappy with some of the school's so-called solutions to bullying too. On one occasion, they had sat Peter with a lower year group, another time they had asked him to help with the library so he didn't get picked on at play time. This just made him feel even more left out."

Matters came to a head at the school play. Peter was Joseph, and after the first show was over, the same children started calling him names and stamping on his feet. Denise says, "He came out from the classroom where they were all getting changed crying, in front of all the other parents, which was very out of character, so we knew it was serious."

After that, Denise and Mike felt that the time had come to take things into their own hands. "The school hadn't stopped the bullying, so we moved both boys to a new school after Christmas. It wasn't entirely straightforward. Our younger son had only spent one term at school, and he hated the thought of starting again in a place where he didn't know anyone. However, it has been the right move for Peter. He only had two terms left at primary school, and felt he had an opportunity to make friends without the same bullies spoiling his chances. The new school has rebuilt his lost confidence, and he was able to move on to secondary school in September a far happier boy."

Meeting your child's needs

One element in choosing a new school will be the response they have to the reason why you are moving schools. For example, if your child has been bullied at their old school, you may want to explain this to the new school, and find out about their policies for dealing with bullying. Their attitude will probably play a key part in your final choice of schools.

How to apply

For most schools, there is a common application form provided by the local authority. Some foundation or voluntary aided schools will have their own form. Check with the local authority or school. You will be able to specify a preference for a number of schools, but you are not guaranteed the place of your choice. The local authority must comply with your preference if possible.

Admission criteria

Schools have criteria for admitting children. This may mean that they give priority to children with brothers or sisters at the school, those who live closest, or those with special needs. Faith schools can give priority to children of a particular faith. The criteria for each school will differ, so it is important to check them for the school of your choice. Admissions criteria come into play if there are more children applying for places than places available.

The criteria are most likely to affect your child if you are applying for a place in reception or starting secondary school. If you are applying to enter in any other year, or even mid term, the criteria will only come into play if there is a waiting list or several children applying for a small number of places. For most applications at unusual times it really comes down to whether there is a place available at all. Each school has an agreed number of places available in each year group and there is often little or no scope for the school to take extra pupils.

Under Fair Access Protocols, children may occasionally be admitted over and above the agreed number of admissions if it won't cause problems for the children already at the school. There are specific rules on class size for classes where children will reach the age of five, six or seven by the end of the school year. There may only be 30 pupils with each school teacher.

Think twice

If you have checked whether the school has places available, and found that they do not, you may want to think again. Similarly, if you would like your child to attend a school that you know will be oversubscribed, look seriously at your chances of getting a place. It may be easier on you and your child to apply to schools which you are happy with and which you have a realistic chance of getting into.

A state school is not allowed to take your child's past behaviour, attendance, attitude or achievement into account when allocating a place, and it may not discriminate against or disadvantage children with special educational needs or disabilities.

Appealing

If you apply for a place at a school and are unsuccessful, you must be given reasons and informed in writing of your right to an independent appeal against the decision. The appeal panel will look at whether the admission criteria were properly applied in your case. If the criteria were not applied properly, then the panel must uphold your appeal unless it affects a significant number of children and would cause problems if they were all admitted to the school. This could be the case if, say, there had been a mistake in calculating distances from school. The panel will then look at whether admitting an extra child would adversely affect the school's arrangements for the year group. Next, the panel must assess whether your grounds for suggesting that your child should be admitted outweigh any prejudice to the school. This is a complex area, and this book can only highlight a few examples. You may want to look at the School Admission Appeals Code for information specific to your circumstances.

HELP AND ADVICE

If you feel you need an independent person to help you with finding a school, you can get advice from The Advisory Centre for Education. An independent advice centre for parents and carers, it offers information about state-funded education in England and Wales for five to 16 year olds. Call their advice line on 0808 800 5793 to talk about all education issues, including exclusion from school, bullying, special educational needs and school admission appeals.

Helping your child settle

Hopefully you have now applied for a school and been allocated the place of your choice. There are several things you, and the school, can do to make changing schools easier for your child. Is it possible to arrange a 'welcome visit' so your child can see the school, visit their new classroom and meet their new teacher? Some schools may have a video about the school for new pupils to watch. You may want to book a meeting with the teacher after the first fortnight to see how your child is settling down.

> Nell and her family bought a new house in the May of her daughter's first year at school. She says, "Dee was in Reception and we didn't want to disrupt her any more than necessary. We found a new school, and visited it with Dee. We went to the school fair too, which gave her the chance to see the building again. The new school suggested that she come along for

the last few weeks of term. This worked well as she got to join in sports day and other end of term events. We invited a little girl over to play after school one day, and I got to know a couple of mums so we could meet over the summer.

"When it came to September, Dee felt less like she was starting a brand new school, and she had friends to sit with from day one. I think it still is a change for her, though. She's gone from a school where she had known some of the children practically since birth, and been to playgroups and nursery together. We're well into her first full term now and she seems to be OK."

Befrienders

Making friends can be hard at a new school, especially for older children. Ask the teacher whether there are any buddy schemes so your child has someone to talk to in the first few days while they find their feet.

DIFFERENT TYPES OF SCHOOL

So far in this chapter we have looked at mainstream state schools. However, there is a range of other options which can suit different children.

Pupil referral units

Local authorities may have a Pupil Referral Unit (PRU). This is a small specialist 'school' which is there to meet the needs of children who because of illness, school phobia or exclusion, for example, cannot attend a mainstream school. There may be a local PRU for school-aged mothers and pregnant schoolgirls.

The hours a child attends a PRU will depend on why they are there. A child who has been excluded may be required to attend full-time, while a child with a long-term illness may only be able to cope with a few hours each week. The PRU may have staff who teach, or may involve external agencies including FE colleges or voluntary organisations. For some children, the aim of time at the PRU may simply be to re-integrate them to mainstream education. Some pupils may attend the PRU on a part-time basis while remaining on the roll of their mainstream school.

Special educational needs

If you are looking for a school which has extra provision for your child's special educational needs, you can go through your local authority as above, or look for independent schools too. There may be a school locally which has special provision for children with particular needs. If there is a suitable local state school, the local authority does not have to support you if you want to send your child to an independent school, a non-maintained special school (run by a charity) or a school in another local authority area.

You can get help from your local Parent Partnership service (in England). In Wales the Special Needs Advisory Project can offer assistance. You can get extra advice and an independent supporter may be able to visit schools with you.

Your options for SEN:

- A unit within a mainstream state school.
- A special school.
- A residential school.
- An independent or non-maintained school. You can pay the

fees for this sort of school yourself, or go through the process to ask the local authority to fund your child at this particular school in order for their needs to be met.

Independent schools

There are many different sorts of independent school. Because of their independence these schools can vary enormously and may be able to offer your child something that is right for them, and outside that offered by state schools. Read on to find out about different theories of education, on which some schools are based, as well as small schools and boarding schools. You can also find out about how to find an independent school, and, of course, how to get any help with fees which may be available.

TEACHING PHILOSOPHIES

In the UK there are two main ways of 'alternative' teaching – Steiner Waldorf and Montessori – that have given rise to a number of educational establishments. Read on for a short introduction to each method, and find out about the new wave of Small Schools which aim to provide for children in a way that larger establishments can not.

Steiner Waldorf schools

This way of teaching is offered in around 35 schools in the UK, for pupils up to the age of 18. There is an emphasis on artistic and practical learning and a focus on the spiritual, physical and moral wellbeing of a child, alongside academic achievement. Formal learning is not forced, with the emphasis on learning in a creative and artistic environment. The school day is focused around the 'main lesson', where a class looks at a subject in depth over three to four weeks, using literacy and numeracy skills as part of their study. In the early years of a child's education, work tends not to be graded, although written evaluations and records may be made.

Steiner Waldorf schools base their teaching on the educational philosophy of Rudolf Steiner.

Christopher Clouder of the Steiner Waldorf Schools Fellowship says, "Steiner Waldorf schools accommodate children from all backgrounds. Our curriculum is artistically structured to respond to the developmental needs of children. This applies to content, art of teaching and timetable. Steiner education respects the essential nature of childhood, enabling children to develop their strengths in a structured and child-sensitive environment." Most Steiner Waldorf schools are fee-paying.

The Steiner approach is not for everyone. Some Steiner schools have been criticised by OFSTED for not placing enough emphasis on basic skills such as reading and writing – although it may be the case that OFSTED inspectors are not sufficiently familiar with Steiner modes of assessment. Victoria Dawson expands on some further issues, "Steiner methods involve story telling rather than reading to the class from a book. Developing a love of books is so important for young children that it seems a terrible shame that Steiner schools aren't using their staff as role models for readers. Staff also only have to attain a Steiner teaching qualification rather than be state-qualified which means that you could be paying to have poorly qualified staff teaching your child. When it comes to secondary education you really do need your child to be taught by specialists in the subject area."

Abigail's daughter, Phoebe, was in middle school when she started to be bullied. Abigail explains, "I think it was because the other girls were starting to get interested in make-up and fashion, swearing and trying to be cool, while Phoebe just wasn't interested. They picked on her verbally, and one day she said she was crouched down in the playground while they all circled round her. We talked to her class teacher and the head, but the school just didn't seem to be able to stop it."

Abigail's husband was initially against the idea of going private, but they decided together to look at the local Steiner school. She says, "We were impressed from the very start. There was a display of woodwork in the front hall of the school: the children had not only made the work, they had made some of the tools too. The school was not academically pushy which was a lovely contrast as Phoebe was in the run-up to SATs and her school seemed to have stopped all the nice activities in favour of preparation for the tests."

Abigail moved Phoebe to the Steiner school at the age of 11 and she immediately settled in. Abigail comments, "It was lovely and inclusive. In the early days they went on a trip: when Phoebe was scared by a horse all the children gathered round to reassure her. The girls didn't mind if she shared interests in fashion – they accepted her for who she was. The classes were smaller and the atmosphere and friendships really helped her build her confidence. There were plenty of trips and activities, so Phoebe got a really broad education. She has gone on to sixth-form college now, but I think would still really prefer to be back at the Steiner school."

Montessori schools

There are around 700 nursery and junior schools in the UK using elements of the Montessori method. Children are allowed to choose their own activities, while observed by the teacher (who may be known as a director). The environment and choice of activities is important in helping the child develop, and should allow children to be independent and discover for themselves. The Good Schools Guide comments that, "The apparent lack of structure can be a problem for some youngsters: others relish the freedom to explore."

Older and younger children share the same classrooms. The Montessori method is based on the child development theories of Maria Montessori, an Italian from the late 19th and early 20th century. She believed that children up to the age of six have limitless motivation to perfect skills, learn and understand things. There is no legal requirement to go through a particular training, so any school can describe themselves as adhering to Montessori methods. Most Montessori schools are fee-paying.

Glen House Montessori is a small school for up to 20 children. The small numbers give the school, "an atmosphere of a 'large family' rather than an institution". As in most Montessori based schools, mixed age groups work together. Unusually, Glen House offers education for children up to the age of 15 who can take two or three GCSEs early before moving on to a sixth-form college to take the rest of their GCSEs in a year.

Children aged two and a half to six attend the Children's House. The Elementary is for children aged six to 11 and the Secondary Group for 11 to 15 year olds. The two older groups often work together. They share the management of the snack shop and have regular school meetings.

Margret Scaife, head of the school, says, "Montessori is the only educational philosophy that gives the children the freedom to learn by following their own interests over the age of six years. Montessori Schools have a unified, internationally developed curriculum, which integrates all areas of development such as physical, intellectual, social, emotional and

> spiritual. The role of the teacher is to stand back and direct the child when necessary. The child will ask the teacher for help, so the teacher will not interfere with the child's work."

Small schools

In the UK there is a number of parent-led projects to set up small schools for anything from six to 60 pupils. Most of these schools operate outside the state sector, so they do not have to stick to the National Curriculum, and are run on democratic principles. The schools try to keep fees low and may do fundraising activities to help with this. Small schools can be particularly good for children who have had problems at their previous school. Many of the schools aim to be environmentally sustainable, and they may offer mixed age learning. Visit the Human Scale Education website to find out more: **www.hse.org.uk**.

> Parents Julie Kelly and Liz Baker founded Great Oaks Small School after their 11 year old children both struggled to cope with the transition to secondary school. Liz explains, "My son joined his secondary school just as it was becoming a technology college. At first we thought this would be great for him: he is dyspraxic and struggles with organisational skills but is quite technically minded. However, it soon became clear that the transition to a tech-based school was far from straightforward for the teachers and assistants, and my son suffered because of this.
>
> The Learning Support Assistants who were supposed to help him deal with his organisation problems had not been trained in the new technology. He was in a laptop-based class. His LSA asked him to bring out his science file, and then shouted at him for trying to access the file on his laptop: she was expecting a folder of papers. There were big issues with homework too.

We counted up to nine different ways that the school had asked for homework to be handed in. We were never clear whether we should be sending in a disk, a worksheet, or uploading a file onto the school's main system. I looked in my son's cupboard one day and found around 50 pieces of work: he had been too scared to hand them in in case he got the format wrong. In the end, he was afraid to go out at weekends and after school in case he ran into fellow pupils and he was having daily panic attacks. I knew we had to do something different."

Liz and Julie took it in turns to home educate their children, and soon found another couple of kids joining them. Once it got to five pupils, they needed to make things more official and so the idea for Great Oaks Small School came about. The school has grown slowly and organically over nine years. It now offers small classes for around 16 pupils studying subjects up to A level. Around half of the pupils are placed by the local authority.

Liz says, "We offer provision for children for whom there is nothing else suitable, filling the gap between specialist and mainstream provision. Children come to us with a range of concerns. Some have been bullied, or simply struggle to cope with the large numbers of pupils in a school. Others have missed chunks of schooling due to illness, and some have mild learning disabilities, poor concentration, or poor co-ordination. In response to this we offer neurodevelopmental exercises every day."

If parents want to get their child into a school like Great Oaks, Liz advises, "Apply to your local authority as soon as possible. It can take 18 months to go through the process, and parents need to be very determined. I would always suggest starting the process before your child gets into Year 9."

Learning is focused on each child's needs. "We try to teach children the subjects they want to learn about. If a child is interested in, say, classical civilization, one of the teachers will adapt and teach according to that child's interests. We have three students in the current sixth form, which means that a lot of one-to-one teaching takes place. We have nine part-time teachers, which allows us to be this flexible."

The school is democratically run. Liz says, "It takes the kids a long time to get their heads round this and understand what is possible. However, two out of the three former pupils who started at university this year have signed up to be year reps, which shows how they appreciate and believe in democracy."

Small schools are, like all schools, inspected on a regular basis. Liz says, "We registered as a school once we reached five pupils. We are now accredited for Key Stage 3 and 16-plus education. We had our Ofsted inspection this year and the inspectors left no stone unturned. We were very pleased with their report."

Independent schools

Independent schools come in many different forms, and can cover primary or secondary age children, or sometimes both. They all charge fees. An independent school is any establishment that provides full-time education for five or more pupils of compulsory school age, or one or more pupils with a statement of special educational need, or in public care, and which is not a school maintained by a local education authority or a non-maintained special school.

Julie made the decision to move her son from a state school to a private school after his first year. She says, "My son is very bright. The school he was attending was unable to keep him stimulated and he began to get into constant trouble. He was withdrawing and becoming unhappy. I found an independent school by looking through the phone book as they did not advertise. I took him for a visit and the atmosphere was lovely. All of the children were polite and engaging. I had visited another school the week before so I was able to compare the two. I was shown some of the work that the children had done and was impressed with what the head teacher said that she could offer my son. I paid a registration fee and sent off the form and I had to wait to find out if there was a place available."

After a stressful couple of months waiting to hear, Julie found that her son had a place. She took him into the school for an assessment, and then had to get him kitted out. She comments, "The uniform cost a small fortune. Private schools can demand that you buy the uniform from a certain supplier rather than at Tesco. The blazer was £45, shirts £12, and trousers were £13 each. On top of this were the school fees, accident insurance, fee protection insurance, the after school activities, and trips."

Julie's son settled in fairly well. She explains, "Starting school was easy for him but it took about a year for him to get used to doing homework. The levels of discipline are far higher in the private sector so I found that he was getting into trouble for minor things but he was getting more attention than he was at his old school and the work was more appropriate to his academic needs.

"I find that there are big differences between the parents so it can be quite hard for a parent to fit in. There are those who you never see because they are working to pay the fees and those who are active members of the school because their partners work so they have lots of free time. A parent is expected to make an effort for the school. Parents are expected to listen to their children read every night and make sure they complete their homework. It is expected that parents attend meetings with their child's teacher unless they have contacted them and rearranged the time. Parents are encouraged to fundraise for the school and to attend their child's plays and concerts, most of which are not free.

"Most private schools have long holidays and it can be hard to find employment to fit around their terms. Holiday clubs outside the school only run during state school holidays so there is often a week or two where there is no holiday care. Then you have to do all of this again when your child moves to a secondary school, which costs more money. At my son's school they are prepared for the common entrance exam, which takes months of preparation. You have to look for a school, register, which costs £75-£150 depending on the school, then the child sits an exam. Then you wait, again, to see if they have a place."

FINDING OUT MORE

Schools belonging to the Independent Schools Council are inspected by the Independent Schools Inspectorate, **www.isinspect.org.uk**. The Independent Schools Inspectorate is a body approved by the Secretary of State for Children, Schools and Families for the purpose of inspecting independent schools as part of the Education Act 2002. Inspections take place every six years, and around 1280 of the more than 2000 independent schools are part of this body. The majority of other independent schools are inspected every three years by Ofsted, in partnership with Cambridge Education, the National Inspection Services Provider for independent schools, and you can find reports on them at **www.ofsted.gov.uk**. Focus Learning Trust looks after the remaining 64 educational charities which are registered as independent schools: these mainly religious school establishments are inspected by School Inspection Services, which is monitored by Ofsted.

Independent schools aren't always the solution for every child, and can vary enormously. Naomi chose her son Neil's school after viewing numerous prospectuses and visiting several schools on a number of occasions. She made her choice of school after being, she says, "impressed by the discipline and old-fashioned morals. The boys have exceptional manners, their respect towards adults is impeccable: they stand when an adult enters the room and wait to be told to be seated, they hold the door open for you and don't push past.

"The classes are small, no more than 18 to a class. Additionally the school has a good reputation for music and sport achievements and we were assured that every boy is given the chance of being on the school sports teams: participation was encouraged over winning. The lunches were prepared in house by a chef from locally sourced fresh produce. Ultimately we felt a good vibe from the school."

Neil has language difficulties which Naomi discussed with the school before starting. She explains, "We were assured that it wouldn't be an issue, as all children develop at different rates and boys identified with SEN receive additional support from the SENCO. He has had 15 minutes a day with the SENCO since starting. But when I asked whether there would be any additional support costs for the next school year, the school suggested that they don't want him there because they believe he's autistic."

Naomi is now looking at other schools. She says, "I've viewed the local state schools but believe that if he's finding it difficult to cope in a class of 12 he won't cope in a class of 30, even with additional one-to-one support as the distractions are too great. We're holding fire at the moment pending the outcome of his assessment by the local autism team and will see what recommendations they make with a view to perhaps being able to use the information to ensure he gets a proper education in a setting that is conducive to his learning. We'd move house again to get him a place in the right school for his needs."

Finding schools: inspections, databases and directories

If you are looking for a fee-paying school you may want to use one of several directories which are now available as books or online. There is no single definitive directory, and not all schools will be listed in all directories. It is worth checking more than one directory to get different views. In some places schools can pay to advertise, while other guides are based entirely on independent assessments: make sure you are clear which you are reading.

- The Independent Schools Council maintains a searchable online directory of schools at **www.isc.co.uk**. It offers links to the inspection reports from the Independent Schools Inspectorate.
- The Good Schools Guide is available as a book and also has a free directory online at **www.goodschoolsguide.co.uk**. It offers in-depth, independent views on over 1000 state and private schools. There is the option to subscribe to the website to see information for schools in the same detail as in the book. They also offer a guide for Special Educational Needs schools.
- The Independent Schools Guide covers in the region of 2000 schools. Most schools are listed by area, with the number of pupils, contact details and fees. Some schools pay for a profiled entry.
- Which School? is a directory of more than 2000 independent schools in the UK, with accompanying website **www.schoolsearch.co.uk**. It also offers directories of special needs schools, boarding schools and 16-plus education. Some schools pay for a higher profile in the guide.
- The Sunday Times Parent Power section has a range of league

tables for independent and state primary and secondary schools:
http://www.timesonline.co.uk/parentpower/league_tables.php

Boarding school

Many parents will not have thought of boarding school as an option. "It costs too much'," or "I couldn't send my child away": there may be many reasons, but boarding school can be exactly right for some children. And nowadays, boarding does not mean that you don't see your child for weeks at a time. Many children now board weekly.

Why board?

There are different reasons to send your child to a boarding school. It may be that you want your child to have some stability if your job, and home, move round the world. As the pupils are in their care 24 hours a day, boarding schools work hard to create a family atmosphere. That can be good for some children who find it hard to fit in. If your child's problems at school actually derive from some kind of problem at home, such as divorce, an alcoholic parent, or a disabled sibling who takes a lot of attention, a boarding school can provide a home-from-home and the chance to get away from the source of the trouble during term time. Hilary Moriarty, National Director of the Boarding Schools' Association, says, "Reasons for going to boarding school include the complete unavailability of a local school which parents think will be suitable or the belief that a child will be better off removed from a particular environment or group of peers."

> Hanford School is for girls aged seven to 13 in Dorset. Rated as 'one of the nicest' girls' boarding schools in the country, it has a range of practices and traditions which have built up over time to ensure that girls feel at home. One way that younger girls are looked after is through the system of committees. The school explains: "The committees are formed by groups of sixth forms ... the committees look after the younger girls and the school. They are helpful and are always looking out for the homesick juniors."
>
> The school arranges clubs and activities at the weekends. "Some children may be involved in matches; others may ride, look after the chickens, swim, climb trees, walk in the hills, play music or organise clubs which are entirely voluntary and are for their own diversion and amusement. These include Art Club, Gym Club, Wiggle Club (dancing), Acting Club, computers and other games. All activities, while organised by the children, are supervised by a member of staff." And birthdays are made special too. "If your birthday falls during term time, your friends will take a pillowcase around the dorms so people can put things in them - maybe writing paper and, if you are lucky, some sweets. Your pillowcase is a little bit like a Christmas stocking."

Boarding may be the only way for your child to access specialist facilities for drama, dance or sport. Hilary Moriarty comments that boarding school may be the solution if parents have "a wish for a child to have more facilities and activities available to them in the evenings and at weekends, or a conviction that a particular school offers a particular service – such as expertise with dyslexic pupils, for instance – which the child needs."

Boarding school may offer children with special needs the help that they need round the clock. New College Worcester, for example, is a residential school and college for young people aged 11 to 19 who are blind or partially sighted. Children study while developing independence skills, including mobility, living skills, and ICT. A residential school can also allow your child with special needs to attend the school that is right for them, even if it is located too far from home to travel daily.

> Hurtwood House is a sixth form boarding school, famous for its performing and creative arts facilities. The Good Schools Guide recommends it for "... the 'I need a change' fraternity and the performing arts enthusiast".
>
> Around a third of the pupils study art and a similar number focus on theatre studies, with input from over a dozen hands-on theatre practitioners as well as visiting professional companies and guest tutors from film, stage and television. Media studies students learn to write, direct, shoot, mix and edit films, music videos, advertisements and documentaries using digital cameras and digital editing suites; they produce radio shows in the school radio station; they learn print and journalistic skills, layout and design, graphics, photography and editorial management and, in the 'new media' they produce web-work to a professional level using industry-standard software.
>
> Headmaster Cosmo Jackson says, "The point about Hurtwood is that it enables the aspiring actor, singer, artist, fashion designer or film director to follow their dreams at the same time as undertaking a full A level programme. What is often overlooked is that Hurtwood is outstanding academically."

Of course, boarding schools vary like any school. Hilary Moriarty says, "A child who is unhappy in a day school, for whatever reason, may find boarding school is exactly the right answer. On the other hand, school for 24 hours a day may feel like a double dose of something a child already hates and it may not work at all. If a child is deeply unwilling to go, boarding is unlikely to work. There are many instances of a child discovering that boarding is a whole different world which suits the child despite their fears or even convictions that they would hate it. But no school will be successful for a deeply unhappy child who may believe he or she has been got out of the way because they are a nuisance or they are unwanted and unloved."

Sarah was at boarding school from the age of six, nearly seven, due to her father's job in Argentina. She says, "My parents decided that a British education was better than the international school in Buenos Aires. They had both been in boarding schools, so I guess they didn't think it unusual. My sister and brother started a year before me at age 10 and eight. I went to the same school as my sister, although we were in different boarding houses so didn't see much of each other. I was happy to go. I guess I just wanted to be like my siblings, but the reality of being away from home was different and I remember feeling very homesick. I left after my 11-plus and went to another boarding school until my parents moved back to the UK when I was 14.

The best thing for me about school was friends. My life was always full of people to hang out with, and the friends I made at school are still friends today. They shared everything with me. They knew about my first period weeks before my mum: she was thousands of miles away! We also had lots to do after school, mostly sports, but at the weekend we did cooking too and we never watched TV. It makes you very independent. At six I could get myself dressed and ready for school with no help. I changed the sheets on my bed, polished my shoes: there were no parents to nag you.

I remember feeling lonely in the holidays because I was away from friends but didn't feel close to my siblings who I didn't see for weeks on end. My parents didn't really know how to discipline me either, so when I went to day school at 14 they let me run riot. My relationship with my family is fine, but we don't have many shared memories from our youth.

I think boarding school suits the more sociable and sporty child, and it works if a parent has problems or if there is an acrimonious divorce maybe, but I won't be sending my kids away – no way."

Finding the right boarding school

Boarding schools vary enormously, and finding the right school for your child is the key. Hilary Moriarty explains, "They may have boarding in common, but they will feel different, be in town or in the country, have weekly boarding available or not, emphasise music or drama or sport differently, be co-ed or single sex, and expect differing levels of academic excellence, and offer differing levels of support for weaker pupils. All this needs exploring with the child before the decision is made. See at least a couple if you can, so that the child feels he or she is involved in the choice, not being 'dumped'."

State boarding

There are 35 state boarding schools in the country, where a parent pays for the boarding element, but not for the education, because it is a maintained school like every other. This means fees are substantially lower than would be the case in an independent school.

BOARDING SCHOOL INFORMATION

You can find information on boarding schools in the independent school directories listed on page 91. For further information on boarding schools and lists of schools and addresses, contact the Boarding Schools' Association, **www.boarding.org.uk**
020 7798 1580.

Help with fees

Figures indicate that between a fifth and a third of all pupils at independent schools get some form of financial assistance with fees. The most common source of assistance is the school itself. Scholarships may be offered to children who show potential in academic subjects, music, art or even sport. Scholarships usually cover up to half the school fees. Means tested bursaries may be available to cover a proportion of the fees, to help parents who could not afford the full fee.

A number of educational charities offer help towards school fees, in certain circumstances. Some focus on particular groups, such as sons of the clergy, while others may offer help to families living in a particular location. Many will offer help towards fees only if independent education is necessary for the child, or perhaps if they would otherwise have to leave a private school due to a change in circumstances. Some may offer grants for school uniform, books, travel expenses, materials for courses, but not help towards the actual fees.

If you have to work abroad, your company may make a grant towards your child's education in a UK boarding school. Similarly, the Ministry of Defence and other government departments may make a grant towards school fees to parents who are posted overseas. Your local authority may occasionally make a grant if they cannot provide an appropriate education for your child: this may be the case if your child has special needs.

The Government offers means tested funding under the Music and Dance Scheme for boys and girls with outstanding talent in music and dance. The scheme helps parents pay the fees and boarding costs at eight specialist independent schools which are centres of excellence in their field. There are means tested grants for part-time dance and music tuition at a number of Centres for Advanced Training around the country. You can find out about these schemes at **www.dfes.gov.uk/mds**, where participating schools are listed. There is also a Choir Schools Scholarship Scheme (**www.choirschools.org.uk**) to help boys and girls from low income families wishing to train at any of the 36 independent choir schools in England.

Ask your local authority's children's services department for information on grant-making bodies in the area, or ask your local library to order the Directory of Grant Making Trusts (£99), which lists bodies that may help you with fees, or The Educational Grants Directory (£34.95). You can also buy both books from **www.dsc.org.uk**.

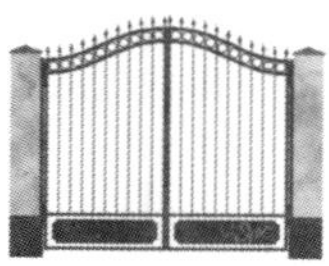

Chapter 5

Home education, flexischooling and tutors

For some children, school is not the right option. They may need a break for a term or more, or you may decide that they are better off learning through home education on a long-term basis. In this chapter, read about how to take your child out of school, and find out how some families home educate their children. You can also read about flexi-schooling and home tutors.

YOUR OPTIONS FOR TAKING A BREAK FROM SCHOOL

You do not have to send your child to school, but you must make sure your child learns at home. Your local authority will check what you are teaching but does not have to help you, and does not offer funding for home education.

Chartered psychologist Dr Paula Rothermel is an expert on home education. She says, "When there are problems with school, when your child is seriously unhappy, home education is a real option. It is not as difficult as it can seem from the outside. To start with, your child can go along with your interests, and they will develop ideas of what they want to find out about. It will help enormously if you are interested in what they are learning. You can then show them how to find things out for themselves. It can take six months to settle into home educating. Rather than feeling you are making a commitment for years, think about trying it for a single school year, then discussing with your child how it is working. This will give you time to develop a routine."

Home education and the law

The legislation which allows you to take your child out of school and home educate differs slightly depending on which part of the United Kingdom you live in. It is also different if your child attends a special school. Read on to find the law that applies to you.

ENGLAND AND WALES

Age four or five or moving area?

In England and Wales, if your child has never been to school, you do not need to notify anyone of your intention to home educate.

Leaving a mainstream school

If you are taking your child out of a mainstream school, you need to write to tell the head teacher what you intend to do. You do not need the school or local authority's permission, and can start to home educate from the date that you notify them. The head teacher will take your child's name off the school register and tell the local authority. See below for an example of a letter you could use: this letter is from the organisation Education Otherwise, which supports families whose children are being educated outside school.

Deregistration letter: from Education Otherwise [**www.educationotherwise.co.uk**]

Your address

Date

Head teacher [name]
School name
Full address and postcode

Dear [head teacher's name]

Re: [your child's name] (date of birth)

After careful consideration I/we have decided to withdraw my/our son/daughter from school in order to take personal responsibility for his/her education. Please delete his/her name from the register in accordance with Education (Pupil Registration) Regulation 8(1)(d) 2006, as he/she is now receiving education otherwise than at school.

Please will you confirm receipt of this letter and inform us of the date that our son/daughter's name was removed from the register.

Yours sincerely,

SCOTLAND

Mainstream state schools

The law is slightly different in Scotland, where you will need local authority consent if your child is currently at a state school. The law states that as far as possible children should be educated according to the wishes of their parents. The local authority will assess the education you propose to provide and base their decision on that. You are entitled to see a copy of what they report.

Other schools

You do not need local authority consent in Scotland if your child has never been to a mainstream state school, or has not been to a mainstream state school in the area you now live in. You can decide to home educate without consent if your child has finished primary school and has not yet started state school, or if their school closes. You can withdraw your child from an independent school without consent.

If you want to adapt the letter, above, the relevant piece of legislation in Scotland is the Education (Scotland) Act 1980, section 30. You should also remember that you may need to ask for consent from the local authority, and could substitute a phrase like:

> I/we would like consent to withdraw my/our son/daughter from school in order to take personal responsibility for his/her education.

To speed things up, Scottish Home Ed support group Schoolhouse [**www.schoolhouse.org.uk**] recommend including an outline of your 'educational objectives' and the resources you will use when teaching your child. The charity also recommends sending your letter by recorded delivery.

NORTHERN IRELAND

In Northern Ireland there is no legal requirement to inform anyone that you are home educating. Much as in the rest of the UK you simply have a duty to ensure that your child receives "efficient full-time education suitable to his age, ability and aptitude and to any special educational needs he may have, either by regular attendance at school or otherwise".

How to deregister

You must deregister your child by writing to the school head, and can adapt the letter above. The legislation for Northern Ireland is the Education and Libraries (Northern Ireland) Order 1986, Article 45.

Support

The Home Ed support Group in Northern Ireland is called HEdNI. They offer an email group, and a website (**www.hedni.org**) with useful resources, articles, and further details on the legal aspects of home education.

Special needs

In all parts of the UK, you will need to ask permission to deregister a child attending a special school. According to S324 of the Education Act 1996 the Local Authority (England and Wales) is obliged to provide for a child's special educational needs unless you make "suitable arrangements" at home: similar conditions apply in Scotland and Northern Ireland. Solicitor Louise Melia of the Education Law Unit in Govan says, "The local authority might have more reasons to object though. They might need convincing that the education being provided at home is suited to that child's additional support needs. Also, if the child receives additional support by way of speech and language therapy, or another kind of therapy at the school, this might be difficult to supply if the child does not attend school (or so the local authority might argue)."

Deregistration letter for a child at a special school: from Education Otherwise and Issie Brookfield of NAS

Your address

Date

Director of Education [name]

Anytown Council

Education Department

Full address and postcode

Dear [name of Director of Education]

Re [Child's name – date of birth – special school attending]

We are writing as the parents of the above named child, who is a child for whom the local authority currently maintains a statement of special educational needs and who is a registered pupil at [name] Special School, [address].

After careful consideration, and following amicable discussions with staff and teachers from the above named school, we have now decided to take full responsibility for providing for our child's education, 'otherwise than at school' in accordance with section 7 of the 1996 Education Act [for England and Wales] OR section 35 (1), and section 37, of the Education (Scotland) Act 1980

We therefore seek the consent of the local authority to allow [child's name] to be deleted from the admission register of the school, in accordance with

Education (Pupil Registration) Regulation 8(2) 2006. Once consent has been given we will provide our son/daughter with an efficient full-time education suitable to his age, ability, aptitude and to his special educational needs.

We look forward to consent for [child's name] to be deleted from the admission register being given to the proprietor of [name] Special School in the very near future and request that confirmation of such action be forwarded to us within the next 14 days.

Yours sincerely,

HE-Special is an email support group for families home educating a child with special needs. It offers a range of articles on the website, **www.he-special.org.uk**. There is a list of parents with home ed experience on the Education Otherwise website's Local Groups page.

Liz took Matt out of school when the school was unable to adapt to meet his needs. Liz says, "I still find it hard to accept that his needs were not met. If he had been blind he would not have been expected to write quickly from the board, so why with dyslexia is he expected to correct something that he has no power over?"

Liz and Matt followed the National Curriculum loosely, adapting it to suit him. Liz says, "Matt is a visual thinker so we did as many field trips as we could. For example, when doing geography, we tracked our local river to its source and took photos all along its path tracking it to the estuary. He looked at erosion and measured flow rates. We have travelled around the UK looking at various landforms, the Lake District, the Peak District and our local coastline. If we could not see something visually we have used clay to understand the concept." Matt has had plenty of opportunity to socialise and play sport too. He plays, teaches and umpires at his local hockey club.

Possible hurdles

Some local authorities may pay more attention to your plans for home education than others. You may be asked to arrange a meeting or the authority may ask for a home visit. You do not have to meet with representatives of the local authority and could, instead, supply them with written evidence of the work you are doing. Remember that it is your choice to home educate your child, and you do not have to justify this to the local authority.

How to do it?

Many parents are daunted by the idea of planning a whole day, or week, or term of schoolwork, but in reality home education is rarely 'school at home'. Dr Rothermel explains, "Children who are home educated are not necessarily trained to sit and study at a desk for hours. Many home educating families spend an hour a day on formal study, some as little as an hour a week. If you are worried about withdrawing your child, don't focus on keeping up with schoolwork. Your role as a home educating parent is to give them the skills to find things out for themselves.

"Your child will learn through all the things they are exposed to that children miss while they are at school. This could be a visit from a man to fix the washing machine, or you may have them with you when you go to the bank or lawyer. One criticism of home educated children is that their language is too advanced for their age, but this is the natural consequence of what they absorb from all these day to day interactions. Life and learning merge after a while."

Your qualifications

You may worry, when embarking on home education, that perhaps you should be a teacher, or have a degree. In fact, no parental qualifications are necessary, just a willingness to help your child and look for resources that will inspire their interest. Join a support group, either online or in your local area, and you will find a whole range of mums and dads who are involved in home education, from different educational backgrounds. Look for Local Groups on the Education Otherwise website: Education Otherwise is happy to accept members who are not yet home educating.

Dr Rothermel says, "Every home educating parent will have moments of doubt whether they are doing the right thing. This can be reinforced by pressure from relatives, other parents and the local authority. If you are even considering home education, join a local group and sign up to an email group. The national email list 'UK home ed' is found at **www.home-education.org.uk**. That way you can find out about your options. You have the support in place if you need.

"There are more other people home educating than you think. You might want to attend a local home ed group before making a decision about what is right for your child. Some parents go along for a day or even try it for a month before making a final decision."

You will probably find that you learn lots of things alongside your child as you study new subjects together. If you don't know where to start when looking into a new subject, ask your local librarian to point you towards some good books on the subject. You will find the library a great resource, and may regularly order and take out books on subjects that interest your child.

Your time

Educating your child at home is a major commitment of your time. Some parents successfully run a business from home alongside educating their children, but many make it their full-time job. If you would struggle financially to do this, could you share home education with another family? Talk to your local Citizens Advice Bureau or Jobcentre and check whether you are getting all the benefits you are entitled to.

What you don't need to do

If you are starting home education, it is helpful to note that you do not need to follow the national curriculum, nor do your children need to take SATs. Don't ignore the curriculum altogether, as it may be a good place to look if you are lacking ideas and inspiration, but you can pull out parts that appeal to you and your children and treat it as one of many useful resources.

You do not need to stick to a 9am to 3pm timetable, or any timetable at all. Learning can take place at any time of the year, which has many advantages. You can plan trips and visits at times when facilities are at their quietest, or choose good weather for outdoor learning.

Do not feel you have to focus on exams and qualifications either. Dr Rothermel says, "Home educated children don't need to do exams at the same time as they would have at school. They may take one or two GCSEs early, in topics which interest them, or do them later. Many home educated children go on to FE colleges. They are self motivated to study from early on. FE colleges are often open to taking on home educated kids and may ask to see a portfolio of work in place of exam passes.

If your child wants to go to university they may choose to go straight to A levels and skip GCSEs. However, they may not decide this until they're in their 20s, when it can be much easier to take A levels."

See Chapters 6 and 7 for more information on GSCEs and A levels outside school, and how older children can opt into exam systems.

Home ed in practice

It can take both parents and children some time to adapt to home education. Think about whether you want to follow an informal system, based on your child's interests, or whether you will all benefit from a timetable. Many families start off with one approach and change as they find what works for them.

> Veronika has educated her daughters at home since they were small. She says, "Life isn't neatly divided into subjects which you drop at the clang of the bell. When we are working on something at home, my daughters might ask if it is science, or art, but the projects we work on cross many areas of learning. We have the freedom to pursue something for as long as the girls are interested, be it three months working on a nature garden, or a question that can be answered in three minutes."
>
> Veronika aims to let her daughters lead the way in choosing what to learn. She says, "At school, learning can be very much controlled by the teacher, and some parents who home educate try to control what their child learns too. But I find many parents fall away from that. Following your child's interests works beautifully. You are always learning something. We talk non -stop if we are walking or shopping. And although we don't go away that often, if I have to give a talk the kids can come with me. We all went to Ireland to tie in with a talk I was giving on home education."

At the age of 11, older daughter Bethany developed an interest in school, so she and Veronika went to have a look. Veronika says, "Initially Eliza, nine, wasn't interested at all, but she changed her mind after Bethany and I paid a visit. Both the girls started school at the start of the summer term. Initially they loved it and were up at six, thrilled to be putting on their uniforms, and experiencing school life like they had read about.

"That soon changed. It wasn't just the morning routine, although we all found it hard to get the girls breakfasted and on the bus. Eliza started to say that she had only had one good lesson that day, and then complained that the following week, because there was a substitute teacher, she didn't even have the lesson she enjoyed. We talked about it, the girls had made friends, but they saw the good things about being educated at home too, and after eight months both girls decided to be home educated again."

Veronika had noticed physical and emotional changes over the time her children were at school. She says, "At the end of the day they just wanted to blob. We had more back chat too. All of that gradually slipped away once they stopped school. I'm no longer the enemy either. While they were at school I enjoyed the time I had to get on with my work, but it feels like we are a family again now. We see each other in all our phases, our ups and downs.

"Now the girls are back to working on home education projects which interest them. They each have a month to find out about a different composer, find a piece of music, and read about his life. At the end of the month each of the girls will present what they have found to the family, and might play some of the music too. I encourage them to look in bookshops and use the library as well as the internet. We don't grade their work, so they don't become emotionally dependent on learning to get good grades or a star. I hope they will learn because they want to learn. My nine year old could tell you anything about the Romans or Jupiter,

> because she has a passion for finding out. When they grow up I hope this will enable them to spend their life doing something they love."

Deschooling

Many home educated children have gone through a time, varying from a few weeks to a few months or longer, of 'deschooling'. This time without formal lessons can help a child adjust to the more flexible approach of home education, and let them think about what interests them, away from a rigid school timetable.

Unschooling or child-led learning

You may also hear people who know about home education mention unschooling, or child-led learning. This is the process where you allow your child to pursue their interests, knowing that they will acquire skills such as reading and writing while, for example, finding out all they can about anything from aeroplanes to Egyptians. Think about how much time you want to spend letting your children learn in this way. It can increase motivation. Some families spend part of the time on projects, which are initiated by the child, and part of their time on basic skills such as reading and writing.

> Helen's daughters were very motivated to work at school, but hard work wasn't seen as cool by their peers. Helen says, "My eldest daughter's problems started in Year 7. She was anxious at lunch times when areas were very crowded, and there was lots of difficult behaviour from other students. It was not directed towards my daughter, but made her feel very uncomfortable with the situation. The staff seemed ineffective, and let the loud mouths be heard, whilst the quieter kids were left behind.

In the end, Helen says, "We decided that school was doing more harm than good for our kids and the way forward was to home ed. The girls were anxious every Sunday evening, and sometimes sick with fear. They couldn't eat breakfast in the morning, were tearful, and even fearful to go out of the house. We took a two-week 'holiday' from school to see how they felt about home ed before informing the schools involved. We sent in a standard deregulation letter, and were slightly surprised that the school didn't even acknowledge receipt of the letter. They simply passed it straight on to the LEA."

Helen has some advice for anyone who is worried about how their child is getting on at school and considering home education: "Get in touch with your school. Don't wait too long for problems to ease – you know your child better than anyone, go with your gut instinct. Get in touch with the LEA and Education Otherwise, go to local home ed groups, speak with as many people as possible to make an informed choice."

Helen's daughters have thrived on home education. She says, "My younger one is relaxed and focused on learning. She enjoys learning music, going to Education Otherwise groups and many other groups. She says she might like to try high school, which we will fully support her with if that remains her choice. Of course, I no longer work as I am at home with the kids so our finances can be difficult. It took the kids a long while to recover, but they have now got a positive outlook on the world and are not fearful of situations."

Staying sane when you home educate

When your child was little, you may have been to mother and baby groups where everyone compared when their children were walking, talking and potty training. It can be the same at the school gate. If you choose to home educate, Dr Rothermel explains, "you have to accept that you are not in the same race as everyone else, and your child doesn't have to jump through hoops at the same time. Some parents will still ask you, 'My son is on level nine, what is yours doing now you are not at school?' You just have to realise that you don't have to compete."

Classes, museums and other trips

You do not have to limit your learning to the home. Open up the home education experience to take advantage of all the resources around you. Can you go to a park or into the countryside to look at plants and animals, or study geology and geography? Are there museums which are full of ideas to help your child find out more about subjects of interest? And are there classes which they might like to join in? Many home educated children play sport in a team or enjoy learning music outside the home. Check out what is available in your local area and see how it can support your home learning.

However many classes you organise, your child will also need to develop some resources of their own. Dr Rothermel explains, "A home educated child needs to be one who is happy with their own company. Even if you organise some shared classes or clubs, there will be times when they need to get on with their own projects while mum or dad works from home, for example."

Groups, camps, conferences and events

You don't have to home educate your child in isolation. There are networks of home educating families across the UK. Look on the Education Otherwise website for a list of local contacts. Local groups will vary in size. There are also occasional camps and conferences which can help inspire and motivate you.

LEARNING ZONE – HOME ED ON THE ISLE OF WIGHT

The Isle of Wight is home to a large home ed group, with up to 65 families as members. In the group, there are around 60 primary age and 60 secondary age children. There are also around eight young adults aged 16 to 19.

Mum of three Bex Smith explains a little about what the group does: "I don't think there is such a thing as a typical month in the Learning Zone (LZ) calendar. Events often follow a seasonal bent and may be organised around what the weather is doing. In the summer we have camps, a cardboard boat regatta, and walks. The winter months have seen a regular weekly club, which offers a variety of activities for all ages of children. It is open to all zone members and we pay subs to cover the hall hire.

There is a LZ choir, made up of parents and children, so we pay for things like our singing teacher to coach us. At the club the kids get to do cooking, music, or drama. A group of older kids are currently working doing a full production of Twelfth Night at a local arts centre, which will count towards two members' GCSE oral exam marks. We have had talks from the local zoo and bat hospital, and a workshop using Fimo which was a great success. LZ members put on an art exhibition in Ryde library which included works of art from all ages. My oldest daughter, Freya, was chuffed to bits that her painting was put up."

Members often use their own talents to teach something to the group. With more than 100 adults taking part there is always someone who has expertise in a particular area. Bex explains, "I took a sewing machine in one week and we did a teddy making session. Another mum took her hand sewing machine, which was great to show the differences between old and new. Some of the kids would have said that they weren't interested in sewing, but with the opportunity in front of them they loved it."

Learning Zone children also get the chance to take part in activities like country dancing, and outdoor games in the playground as the club is held at a large youth centre. Bex says, "In the summer this particular club will quite probably make way for other activities that are much more outdoors based." The group also holds a monthly committee meeting and an annual AGM, in order to meet requirements of being a registered charity.

Parents and children both get a lot out of being part of the Learning Zone. Bex Smith again: "It is not just the social side. The first thing that a non-HE person will ask is, 'How on earth do they get enough social interaction when not in school?' In reality they get far more, with children and adults from all walks of life, and all ages; currently my children have friends who are aged from two right through to 15 plus, and they get on well with all of them, and they're friends with many adults too. They get to work with other children, and have the opportunity to do group activities and projects.

"As a parent, I get loads from being a part of the Zone too. The community feel is fantastic. I know parents who share similar aims to my own, who I can share experiences with, can look to for advice and suggestions if I am unsure which way to do something, or even look to for inspiration if my children want to do something which is beyond my knowledge or experience. As one example, my middle son, Ferdy, has said he wants to learn to play trumpet. We have one, but don't know how to play. I chatted to a dad at our weekly club who plays a few brass instruments and he is happy to help Ferdy get started.

"A group of parents has got together in the last few months and created our own band which will provide music for some ceilidh dances at the Christmas party. If there are other things going on around the Island then families may get involved as a result of the information being spread through the LZ grapevine. LZ is more than just a group of home educators, invariably it becomes a group of friends who are there on many levels."

Bex joined the group within a couple of months of moving to the island, "My youngest, Felix, was just nine days old, and it was our first outing from the house. I was daft enough to put my hand up when they wanted someone to do the newsletter, and I have to say that jumping in at the deep end has definitely been worth it. I am not normally good at putting myself forward: self-confidence has always been a major issue for me. Two years on I feel very much a part of the Zone, my own self-confidence has grown, as well as my confidence in my ability to provide enough interest and variety for my children to learn what they need to at least in these early years of their 'school' life.

"The reports I have had from our local EOTAS [Education Other Than at School] lady have been very positive, and make it sound like we do loads more than I ever give myself credit for doing with the kids. "

Home educating in a family

It is very common to home educate one child while others go to school. A child who is happy at school will not thank you for taking them out, even if you are home educating a sibling. Children who are home educated may ask at some point to opt back in to school, perhaps because they want to try secondary school. Home education is enormously child centred, so children usually get the choice to go to school if they want. It is rare for a child to be exclusively home educated up to 18.

Cost

All this talk of trips and classes may make you worry about the cost of home education. There is no financial support from local authorities towards home education, and the time commitment can leave two-parent families relying on a single income. Single parents can feel stretched trying to juggle looking after a child and earning a living, while any parent may occasionally wish for the respite that school used to offer. With time, you will get to know how to keep the cost of home education manageable.

Make the most of libraries and free museum entry. Friends and family can be a valuable, yet free, source of expertise in different areas and may be delighted to help an interested youngster who wants to hear all about something they share a passion for. You will also get to know which resources you have to pay for, and can stock up on paper and art materials in the sales. The internet offers an enormous range of resources. You may want to subscribe at home, or make use of free internet access at your local library.

Home education can lead you to take a fresh look at how you live. Many parents who home educate are committed to a healthy lifestyle. Growing vegetables and cooking meals from scratch can be part of the learning experience for your child, and help you keep your budget under control too. And finally, of course, you can take holidays at times which suit you, avoiding costly school holidays. House swaps may be a good way to get time away without breaking the budget.

Flexischooling

Before you go all out for full-time home education, you may want to look into flexischooling. This approach allows a child to remain registered at a school while having time out to meet their needs. This can work for a child who has problems with a full-time school day due to health issues or school phobia, or may work well for parents who feel that the school is not meeting their child's needs in some way.

The parent agrees with the head and class teacher that the child will attend school for, say, mornings only, either indefinitely, or for a term or year. This approach relies on the agreement of the head, and will only succeed if the class teacher also is committed. Otherwise, a child can end up feeling that they are missing out on part of school life. You may want to spend the time your child is not at school doing some one-to-one study, or different activities. You will need to talk to the school about a co-operative approach to covering the same curriculum.

If you need help to convince the school, you need to quote Section 444 of the Education Act 1996 which explains how the school can deal with 'irregular attendance' in England and Wales. The Act makes provision for leave to be granted from school by "any person authorised to do so by the governing body or proprietor of the school". There is no such provision in Scottish law, but of course that does not mean that you could not discuss flexischooling with a co-operative teacher.

Tutoring

Many parents do not feel that they know enough to teach their own children. You may feel well equipped to help with some subjects and not others. A home tutor could be just what you need to get some external input. This individualised help comes at a price, of course. The Good Schools Guide quotes prices ranging from £15 to £60 per hour.

Finding a tutor

Tutors do not have to have specialist qualifications – anyone can advertise their services, so you may want to ask about their previous experience and qualifications. There are lots of online directories too: find out whether they simply act as central check point for tutors' qualifications and certificates, or whether they meet and interview each tutor. Get references, or a personal recommendation. You may want to look for someone who has a current CRB check (a check that they have no criminal record). If your child wants to take specific exams or qualifications, make sure the tutor is familiar with the requirements.

Beyond the basics, and perhaps most importantly, you also want someone who can inspire and challenge your child. If you meet the tutor by yourself initially, it can be worth meeting them with your child too, so you can see how they get on. If you go through an agency, do insist on meeting the tutor before committing to anything. Look out for free introductory lessons, and you may want to shop around before signing up to a long series of lessons.

What to ask

Find out what resources the tutor provides, and what they will want you to supply in the way of books or computer facilities. How often do they suggest meeting your child and what work will they set for completion in between? Ask how they will keep you up to date on your child's progress.

> Rosie took her son out of school and arranged for him to go to a number of tutors. She explains why: "After Tom's father died, he managed to hold everything together, just, until he took his 11 plus. I think he just let go emotionally after that, and his behaviour at school deteriorated. We'd had

intermittent behaviour problems for years because he's very bright and has Asperger's. This time the school handled it badly and Tom was in no state to cope.

"He'd been seen for years by a wonderful clinical psychologist and she came to the school with me and explained that their approach was likely to make things worse, and outlined techniques that could help. His form teacher was hugely supportive, but the head teacher refused to budge and insisted that bad behaviour must always be punished. I just couldn't bear to see him so miserable, and his behaviour at home was dreadful as a result of all the stress. As he had only two terms of Year 6 left to go I decided to get him out of school before he became any more unhappy."

Rosie had a friend who was a maths tutor who put her in touch with other tutors. She says, "I organised a timetable for Tom which involved 15 tutors in all. We met them all to ensure Tom got on with them. He spent three hours each morning split between two tutors. I picked him up at 12.30 and in the afternoon a tutor would come to the house. I looked for people who weren't bound by conventional approaches to teaching as Tom thrives on the stimulation of doing things differently – day visits, field trips and plenty of variety.

"We started with a good range of tutors, with a bias towards Tom's favourite subjects, but over the two terms a couple left and I added one or two. In the end he studied maths, science, biology, English, drama (he took his LAMDA grade exams), history, geography, Chinese, cookery, touch typing, IT (he built his own website), animation, natural history, gardening, music (mostly studying film scores), art, design technology, circus skills, martial arts, tae kwon do and squash.

"The best tutors were the ones who steered clear of the conventional 'sit down with a workbook and pencil' approach and went for more novel ways of teaching. I can certainly say that Tom learned far more about a wide range of topics than he would have done if he'd stayed at school. And he was blissfully happy – countless people commented on what a different child he was, not just from the months leading up to taking him out of school, but different from how he'd been for years.

Rosie found using tutors expensive, but was able to do it for the six months until Tom started at grammar school. She says, "The tutors mostly charged around £23 an hour and he had four and a half to five hours tutoring a day. I reckoned that this worked out at about the same cost as a good public school, and less than some.

"The biggest problem was that tutors would occasionally phone or email and say, 'Sorry, I can't do this week'. I remember one week when five of them pulled out. That was a nightmare to reorganise as Tom got very bored if his day wasn't reasonably full. If I did it again I would have fewer tutors covering more topics each. Another difficulty was that although I work full-time from home, there are times when I need to be out or away. I'd been used to the boys being at school from 8.30 to 4.30, but suddenly I had a child at home in the middle of the day who was too young to be left unsupervised."

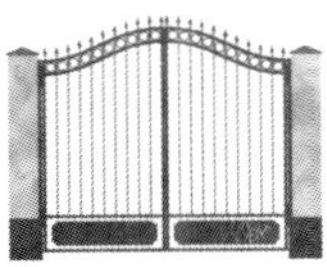

Chapter 6

Education 11–16

Entering secondary school can bring up a range of new challenges. Some kids relish the greater freedom, but for many a bigger school can seem overwhelming. The pressure starts to grow to pass exams and make life choices too. Read on to find some different ways to approach these challenges. This chapter also looks at the types of bullying that are more likely to crop up at secondary school and how to deal with it.

THE FIRST YEARS OF SECONDARY SCHOOL

Children in the first few years of secondary school may find themselves learning in a very different way from before. There will be tests, more homework and ongoing assessments. Some children struggle with the increased academic demands. Here are some ideas to help them keep up:

- Make a routine. Find your child a quiet place to study and help them to do their homework at the same time every day. You may need to be available for encouragement.
- Keep younger siblings entertained with a quiet activity at this time to support your older child.

- Some children may not know where to start. Maybe they want to start with something difficult to get it out of the way. Doing an easy piece of work first can help a child get going, but you may need to make sure that the harder stuff is done next.
- Find out which homework has to be in when to help them prioritise.
- Ask the teacher how long they should be studying for each evening. Most children are tired at the end of the day, so keep the time spent on homework to a manageable level.
- Sometimes it is better to take a break from a big piece of work and try again later.
- Know when it is time to stop. A child can make less and less progress as it gets later in the evening. Occasionally it may be best to tell them to stop, even if you have to explain to a teacher why they could not complete the work.
- Allow time for your child to relax and wind down. Have a chat over a piece of toast about how the day has gone, or play some games to make a break between homework and bedtime. A good night's sleep makes it easier for them to do well at school the next day.
- Be interested in their work. Talk about what they are studying. If they are interested in a topic help them find library books or websites, or take the family on a relevant trip. Ask the teacher for ideas to help your child in subjects where they struggle
- Praise your child whenever you can. This might be for great results, or for sticking at something they find hard.

SECOND STAGES

From Year 9 your child will be making choices about their future. They will need to decide which GSCEs to take. This decision can seem overwhelming at the age of 13, and there can be enormous pressure to get it right. Most schools will require your child to take a core of subjects including maths and English and science, and your child may be left with only a small range of choices.

Career choices

Now is a good time to explore career choices with your child. Many children at this age have little or no idea what they want to do. While it can be useful to look at which subjects will help them in later life, they also need to know that it is worthwhile picking subjects that they enjoy. And it is entirely possible to study for an additional GCSE later in life if needed. It is one of those areas where many people will look back and wonder what all the stress and pressure was about when, a few years down the line, interviewers rarely if ever want to know about GSCE subjects or even results.

There are other options too. You child may prefer a more vocational BTEC or OCR Nationals course in subjects like art and design, business, health and social care, science or sport. Some schools can offer these courses at age 14 to 16 alongside courses in Key Skills such as English and maths.

Doing it differently

If your child is struggling at school or you are considering home education, you may be worrying about GCSEs and A levels. Don't feel that there is only one way to succeed in life, which involves passing several GCSEs in one sitting at school. There are other routes which still allow your child the possibility to go on to further or higher education, or into vocational training to do something they enjoy. In England, a new Diploma for 14 to 19 year olds is being rolled out, and will combine literacy and numeracy with skills for life and the option to focus on a vocational area such as engineering in a practical way.

Matt has dyslexia and studies at home. He decided to take GCSEs in physics, chemistry, biology, geography, English, maths and ICT. His mother, Liz says, “We were lucky enough to find Sheffield College online learning. They have inspired him and turned around his previous failure at Key Stage 1 and 2 to find that although dyslexic he is talented at English.

“From dreading having to do English at GCSE, he has been nurtured to develop a love of writing and carried on to A level. His educational psychologist also suggested that he did a touch typing course at the Helen Arkell Centre which has made life so much better for him when writing for English. I’m delighted that he obtained excellent grades for all his GCSEs and is now taking four AS levels.”

Correspondence courses

It is possible for children to study remotely, using the post, email and the internet to enable them to learn, submit work and have it assessed. There are a small number of providers who offer Key Stage 3 courses for 11 to 14 year olds, as well as GCSE and A level courses. This sort of provision can be a boon to any parent who wants help in deciding what to study, and in delivering it.

Key Stage 3

At Key Stage 3 there is a limited range of distance learning subjects available, including maths, English and science and history. There are many more subjects available if you look in a bookshop, and of course at this stage you do not need to be restricted to the Key Stage course. However, if you are thinking of entering your child for GCSEs it can make things easier if they have gone through the Key Stage 3 work first.

Jenny Langmead, head of Little Arthur School, says, "GCSE courses rarely spend much time on elementary principles. The usual outcome of this is that the child gets frustrated and soon gives up. I do think it's important that parents take a longer term view of where they're going with home education. If they and their children want to reject formal exams, fine, but, if they hope to equip their children with GCSEs, it's far less painful to slowly work through Key Stage 3 topics during the 11 to 14 period."

> Little Arthur School is an independent school on the Isles of Scilly, geared exclusively to the needs of home educated children. Head teacher Jenny Langmead says, "We offer a service to parents who really want to provide the same sort of education that their kids would get at school. For 11 to 14 year olds we offer English, maths and science. Families who sign up get sent a file of work. You need to work through each part with your child and then send in an assignment. We suggest you aim to complete one assignment each month, but some families complete the whole file in six months while others take three years. It is important to work with your child at this age. They do not yet have the motivation to just get on with it by themselves."
>
> Services like that offered by Little Arthur can help parents who are unsure about educating their child themselves. Jenny explains, "When you send in

the assignment you get the feedback to reassure you how your child is getting on. If you're stuck, we can send help sheets, and we can share with you examples of the sort of work your child should be aiming for. Parents can find it very hard when faced by a wall of books in a book shop to know what to choose: our courses make it easier. It can be difficult to assess your child's work too."

Jenny set up the school when home educating her children, in response to the lack of support available for parents. She explains, "We don't offer 24-hour a day support or online provision, because we are aiming to keep the costs down. Our Key Stage 3 courses cost in the region of £105, and IGCSEs cost around £145. If you have more than one child you can photocopy the worksheets and simply pay for extra marking."

Older children can study University of Cambridge International GCSEs through Little Arthur. There is a wider choice of subjects, and by this stage children may be more motivated to study. They are sent text books and 10 to 12 assignments. After that they can complete a mock exam, and further exam practice is available if needed.

GCSEs

A range of distance learning subjects are available for GCSEs. You may need to opt for courses which are assessed by examination rather than coursework if you are studying from home. It is harder to study experimental subjects like physics and chemistry without lab facilities, but some providers have adapted the courses so these subjects can still be taken. If you are thinking of entering your child for GCSE courses, it pays to plan ahead.

Jenny Langmead says, "Many parents are unaware of the actuality of taking IGCSE exams: both the cost and the time involved in locating an exam centre and in registering for exams. Because children in school do not pay for exams, the cost often comes as a shock. Also, a lot of parents fail to appreciate that exams need to be registered for a long way in advance. Many people find it hard to locate an exam centre which will accept them. A lot of correspondence courses offer to mark course work. Unfortunately, they don't point out that exam centres are often unwilling to accept course work set and written by teachers not in the school. Parents really need to be aware of the pitfalls when considering exam options."

Examples of GSCEs available by distance learning include:

- Additional Science
- Biology
- Business Studies
- Chemistry
- Child Development
- Economics
- English Language
- English Literature
- French
- Geography
- History
- Information & Communication Technology
- Law
- Mathematics
- Physics
- Psychology
- Science
- Sociology
- Spanish

Some distance learning providers

Edexcel: Provides IGCSEs which home educated children can take as private candidates – **www.edexcel-international.org** 01204 770696.

Oxford Home Schooling: GCSEs and Key Stage three and A levels – **www.oxfordhomeschooling.co.uk** 0800 0111 024.

The Sheffield College: English at GSCE and A Level by online learning – **www.sheffcol.ac.uk** 0114 260 3603.

National Extension College: GCSEs and A levels – www.nec.ac.uk 0800 389 2839.

Little Arthur Independent School: Key Stage three and IGCSEs – **www.littlearthur.org.uk** 01720 422457.

Checks and accreditation

You should make some checks before paying for a distance learning course. Look for colleges which are accredited by the Open and Distance Learning Quality Council (ODLQC). Check exactly what qualification is being offered and whether there is a refund policy. Make sure you are clear about the level of tutor support and whether this will be enough for you and your child. You may want to ask to see an example of course materials before signing up, or get recommendations from satisfied students.

Local FE colleges

If your child has reached 16 and needs a GCSE in a fundamental subject like maths or English, your local college of further education is likely to have these courses on offer. They are less likely to make the courses available to under-16s, but check with the principal as this decision is up to them.

> Emily is studying GCSE German, English, and maths through a distance learning company. It sends all the materials and marks course work but does not provide exam venues. Mum Helen says, "We have to find an exam venue that is wiling to accept private candidates and of course pay the costs involved."
>
> Emily is also studying at home for IGCSEs in biology, French, history and geography. Helen explains, "These are much more straightforward. We purchase books from any bookshop for approx £16 and then pay a further £99 to a company who provide the exam venue in either Bristol or London. Had we realised this option was available, we probably would have taken this route for the other subjects too. IGCSEs are recognised by colleges here in the UK. Just like GCSEs you need five with a pass mark of C or above to gain a place. We have recently found out that some colleges take students without GCSEs. Instead they offer an interview as selection. It is interesting should you not want to go down the GCSE route. It seems much of a postcode lottery though, as some of ours offer that and others not."

BULLYING FOR BIG KIDS

There are some sorts of bullying that happen mainly to children at secondary school. This section gives you some pointers if your child is being subjected to cyber bullying or racist or homophobic bullying.

Cyber bullying and mobile phone abuse

It can be very frightening to receive a threatening phone call, text or email, and unfortunately children can find themselves being bullied in this way. Some may have rude or abusive posts made about them online. It can seem hard to know what to do to solve the problem, but a lot of the messages or posts will be illegal, and the police, phone company or internet service provider can work with you to get the bullying stopped.

Net names

If your child gets an abusive email, tell them not to delete it. Contact the company providing the sender's email facilities (such as Hotmail) with details of the email. Even if the sender is using an anonymous email address, the company can use information contained in the email to track them down.

Website gossip

If a website is displaying rumours or abuse about your child, get in touch with the internet service provider. The company hosting the site can find the owner and ask them to remove the problem content, or take down the site.

Phone abuse

If your child is on the receiving end of silent calls or gets threatening messages, note down when the calls took place and what was said. If a message is left, keep that too. This provides the police with evidence of harassment. Even if the caller is anonymous, the police can get mobile phone service providers to find which phone a call was made from. The simplest way to protect your child in this situation may be to change their phone number by buying another SIM card

TIPS FOR YOUR TEEN

Help your child to stay safe by chatting about the following tips:

- Don't give out personal details online.
- Only answer phone numbers you recognise.
- Just say 'hello' when you answer your phone and leave the caller to say who they are.
- Share your phone number only with people who need to know it.
- Don't flash your phone in public.
- Show abusive texts or email to your parents.

Homophobic and racist bullying

Make sure your child is clear that no one has the right to call them names. The Equality Act (Sexual Orientation) Regulations 2007 outlaw discrimination against pupils on grounds of their sexual orientation. This means that schools must deal with bullying on grounds of actual (or perceived) sexual orientation as seriously as bullying on grounds of race, gender, disability, religion or belief, and age.

It is easy for the usual cliques and friendships that form in school to turn into bullying, sometimes on the grounds of race. Equal opportunities consultant Kamaljeet Jandu says, "The heads and leaders of any school need to clearly state their zero tolerance of bullying, in particular racist bullying. They need to employ a programme of awareness raising with teachers, Governors pupils and the parents. The awareness raising should include:

- What is racist bullying
- Acceptable and unacceptable behaviour
- Clear system of redress
- Possible penalties if proven guilty

"All new pupils and parents should be made aware of racist bullying and potential disciplinary measures."

> Bexhill High School has been working to improve the way students treat each other and members of the local community in and out of school. Student support co-ordinator Trudy Hillman says, "Two students approached us, concerned about racist comments which were from fellow students, mainly outside school. In school there were clear ways to report and deal with racist bullying, but it was less clear to the students what they could do outside school."
>
> Bexhill High has relatively few students from ethnic minorities, which could have left them feeling isolated. Instead, the school decided to use Anti Bullying Week to tackle the issue head on.
>
> Hillman explains, "Students ran an experiment where some kids were given a red card and others a green one. With the assistance of senior staff they explained that those with green cards could come in later, go home earlier and go first in the dinner queue. This led to a discussion in assembly about how students felt being discriminated against based on a colour. This was backed up by activities in form time to carry on the message. Students looked at what had happened in Rwanda, for example.
>
> We also ran a Football Against Racism tournament, which got the message to a different group of students. The student leadership body, about 100 students, were out and about with flyers to engage younger students in discussion about racism and its impact."

> Since that week in October, Hillman says, "the school has been looking together at how we want people to treat each other. Students have been working together in form time to come up with ideas which will become a charter. We are asking questions like, 'If your mum came into school, how would you like people to treat her?' Pupils have been sharing experiences of racism in class. Every student has been given small tasks to do on a daily basis over a period of two weeks. One day we asked them all to hold a door open for someone, on another to smile at a stranger. We then talk about the response they got."

Some children may be bullied and called 'gay' or subjected to other homophobic attacks. Nigel Tart of Schools Out says, "Unfounded fear of Section 28 led most schools to censor LGBT [Lesbian, Gay, Bisexual or Transgender] issues from the curriculum. Many teachers even believed it prevented them from challenging homophobic bullying. Even now, most teachers are unaware of their legal responsibilities to create a safe and supportive learning environment."

Tart continues, "The period between self-identifying as LGBT and coming out to other people (on average two or three years) makes LGBT young people particularly vulnerable. Homophobic and transphobic bullying usually goes unreported – partly because the target knows little will be done about it, but mainly because of the stigma attached to LGBT identities. Parents shouldn't assume their children will confide in them. Kids are bombarded with cultural homophobia every single day, so even a throwaway comment about a gay TV character can jeopardise their confidence in you.

Also, don't forget: many straight kids experience homophobic bullying too and are just as likely not to confide."

The Schools Out website [**www.schools-out.org.uk**] contains model anti-bullying and equal opportunities policies with guidelines for their implementation, as well as a Student Toolkit for dealing with homophobia and transphobia. Tart concludes, "Anti-bullying measures are essential, but schools really need to proactively challenge the stigma by reintroducing LGBT issues into the curriculum. LGBT History Month (every February) is an excellent starting place, and **www.lgbthistorymonth.org.uk** has some excellent education resources."

Both racist and homophobic bullying should be included in a school's anti-bullying strategy. School staff need to be committed to develop, implement and monitor the policy. Citizenship lessons can help children look at how to beat prejudice and discrimination. There is a history of reticence when it comes to addressing lesbian, bisexual, gay and transgender issues in schools. Children may only come across the subject in a negative way when discussing sexually transmitted diseases in PSHE classes.

As well as Schools Out, Stonewall has a range of materials to help students and schools at **www.stonewall.org.uk**. There is advice on dealing with bullying on the Equality and Human Right Commission website at **www.equalityhumanrights.com**.

MORE HELP

Get more help and advice about stopping bullying from BullyingUK [**www.bullying.co.uk**]. Your child can also call Connexions Direct for free confidential advice on almost any issue relevant to 13 to 19 year olds, from health to studying - 08080 013 219 **www.connexions-direct.com.**

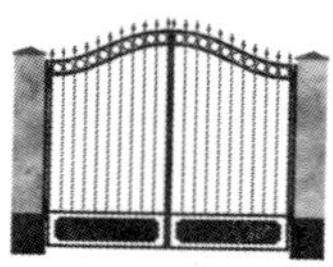

Chapter 7

Education post 16

In some ways, it becomes easier to deal with school problems after the age of 16. School is no longer compulsory. But what do you do if your nearly adult child is keen to continue their education, but experiences problems while they are learning?

PARENTING PRINCIPLES

Parentline Plus has some great principles for dealing with teenagers, based on freedom, love, listening, privacy and setting boundaries. It is difficult to negotiate the fine line between letting teens have the freedom to make their own decisions, and setting enough boundaries for them to feel cared for. Teenagers will often want to make decisions alone, even if they then need your help to deal with the consequences. Setting careful boundaries can help them make choices safely. Show them that you feel that their thoughts matter. Listen to their views, and practise negotiating outcomes that work for both of you. Bear these ideas in mind and they will help when you and your 16 or 17 year old are negotiating your way through further education. Visit **www.parentlineplus.org.uk** for more help.

Your teen's options

Most 16 year olds will have looked at their options while in Year 11 and already have ideas about whether they want to continue to study, and where. The usual options include:

- continuing at their current school
- moving to a different school
- moving to a local sixth form college or further education college

Teenagers can also opt for A levels or choose work-related qualifications such as BTECs, City & Guilds and OCR Nationals. Different schools and colleges offer different balances between vocational and academic courses.

Starting college

If your teenager has made the choice to study full-time and passed the GSCEs they need to get into the college they want, you hope that everything will be straightforward. There can be teething problems in the first few weeks. College work can be very different. It can take even the quickest student a while to adapt to the requirements of an A Level course. There are social challenges too. At a new college it can take time to find friends, and even at the same college different subject choices can mean that old friends don't often meet. If your teen is still struggling to make friends, encourage them to join clubs either at college or outside. Most colleges offer a range of different activities one afternoon a week where students get a chance to mix with new people and meet others who might share similar interests.

Study troubles

Whatever the teething problems, encourage your teenager to try things out for a few weeks, Find out if there is a parents' evening or other opportunity to discuss things with staff to sort out academic issues.

Changing course

Sometimes it won't be apparent until term starts and students are discussing their courses that there may be new and different subjects to study. It may be possible to change courses, especially if this is flagged up as early as possible, and this can make all the difference to how your child feels about studying.

Many colleges get students to take four AS levels, with the idea of dropping one subject at the end of the first year. If your child is struggling academically, they may want to drop one subject sooner to focus on doing well at the others. Check that the remaining subjects leave their options open for future career choices. Go back to Chapter 3 for more tips on working through issues with the school.

> Stephanie says, "I was studying geography, photography and art. I didn't enjoy the first year. I'd found there was a lot of work and not enough time to do it. At secondary school with one lesson after another you were consistently busy, but there were lots more gaps between lessons, so I found it hard to get back into concentrating when I needed to. By the end of the year I was ready to leave."
>
> Her mother, Sarah, continues the story, "We decided we needed to speak to the tutor before Stephanie decided to leave. We wanted to check they

thought it was worth her going back, and to make sure that she was capable of doing the exams. The tutor was helpful and said it would be a shame to give up now."

Stephanie says, "I didn't want mum to phone my tutor at the time, but it did help, because the tutor hadn't been aware that I was so unhappy. He talked to me about planning my work, and giving myself time for study and time for fun. He suggested I didn't work on Sunday, say, and took one evening off, while setting free periods aside to do my work."

Sarah says, "That was great advice which came better from the tutors than from us as Stephanie's parents."

Stephanie also changed from studying photography to geology, which she preferred. She comments, "It was hard going, and I still felt like leaving at times. It was difficult at Christmas because the exams were coming up, and even after I got my results I didn't feel very motivated as I felt lots of my friends had done better."

Mum Sarah says, "We tried to break it down for Stephanie, and said, 'Go back in September and try it for six weeks until half term.' Then, we persuaded her it wasn't that long if she stayed and completed the term. Once we'd made it through Christmas it was really only one more term, and then it wasn't so hard to persuade her that it was worth doing the exams. I was a bit worried what would happen if we persuaded her to go back and she failed in the end, but that didn't happen."

Stephanie and her mum both agree that they are really pleased she hung in there and got grades that she was happy with. "I carried on and in the end I passed all my subjects. I'm pleased I have some qualifications and can go to uni if I want."

A levels are not the only option

Education in a school or college setting is not right for everyone. If your teenager is continually complaining about college, take a step back. Ask them why they chose to go, and what they would like to do in the future. It may be that college is necessary in order to achieve a career, or simply somewhere to go while they are working out what they want to do. Are they there because they want to be, or are they there because you expected them to go on to further education, regardless of their interests? Look again at their choice of course too.

> Eleanor is now 22 . At 16 she was quite clear about the career she wanted. She says, "I've been riding since I was eight or nine, and I knew I wanted to work with horses. I didn't see the point of doing A levels, but Mum and Dad were really keen. We came up with a compromise. I was down for one A level at my old school, one at an evening class, and my parents had agreed that I could spend the rest of the week training to become a riding instructor.
>
> "Going back to school part-time was awful, and I really wasn't interested in the evening class either. It was easy to skip classes and after the first term I just didn't go back at all. I'm now a qualified instructor. I run my own business and am fully booked for riding lessons every week, but I never completed the A levels."

Further ed, further away

There is scope to go away to study at this age, with financial assistance available if the course is not on offer within 15 miles of home. You can find out about applying for help with accommodation and travel costs under the Residential Support Scheme funded by the Learning and Skills Council. The grants of a few thousand pounds a year are based on household income and are available for up to three years.

Tom chose not to go on to study A levels but made the most of the options on offer to him to get started in a career in sport and leisure. He says, "I have dyslexia and swapped schools before GCSEs so I could take more practical subjects. After GCSEs I stayed on in the sixth form. My school offered a diploma of vocational education (DVE) so I took that alongside three more GSCEs at evening class.

"I'd really got into canoeing and wanted to do an outdoors course, but you have to be 17 or 18 to do many of the instructors' courses, so I felt a bit like I was filling in time doing the DVE. It was the first year the school had run the course and there were lots of people who were doing it because there was nothing else they wanted to do. Students kept missing deadlines for work, and the staff kept extending the deadlines. It all became a bit demotivating.

"There were some really good things at the school. The youth worker did an awful lot to help me organise things that I was interested in like going caving, canoeing or taking part in the Duke of Edinburgh's Award scheme. The careers office was a good resource too. They helped me find out about outdoor pursuits courses.

"I ended up working three or four days week to save up so I could go away to Bicton College of Agriculture in Budleigh Salterton to do a BTEC national diploma in outdoor leisure. That was brilliant. It gave me lots of insights into different areas. There was a bit of finance and accounting, marketing, and we learnt about websites. There was a good work placement too where I worked in a sports centre as a canoe instructor.

> "The tuition fees were paid by the council, and I got some help from a grant and my parents towards my accommodation. I'd saved up enough to get through the first year, and the college accommodation was cheap. By the end of the second year I was £1000 overdrawn but that wasn't bad."

Other ways to get qualifications

At 16 it is possible to get qualifications without attending school or college five days a week. If your teenager's study arrangements aren't working out, here are some alternatives:

Further education colleges

FE colleges have many courses on offer which can be studied on a part-time or evening basis. Courses are generally free for 16 to 18 year olds. Your teen may prefer to have a part-time job and study part-time at a FE college.

Day release

If your teenager is interested in a vocational career there are advantages to looking into studying on a day release basis. They get practical experience plus training, and the chance to try out new skills in the workplace.

> Helen says, "I didn't want to stay on after school, but fancied trying hairdressing. I got a job and spent one long day a week at college. I enjoyed the training, but the salon I worked in was awful. I didn't feel I was earning anything, rarely got the chance to practise what I was learning at college and usually got left just to clean up.
>
> "I talked to the college. They were fairly helpful and suggested I looked round for other jobs. However, they were quite clear that it was essential

that I had a job as it was part of the course requirements, and suggested I should stay at the salon until I found something else. It wasn't easy to find another job, especially as most of my time was spent working and studying. Mum and I looked around and eventually I found somewhere else to work where they would also let me do my training. It was much better as, although I still needed to sweep up and make the coffee, the owner made the time to ensure I got to practise too."

Evening classes

Taking a range of evening courses can give independent teens the freedom they want. Being part of a class of adult learners will bring them into contact with people with a wider range of experiences and different attitudes to studying, which can be helpful. Your teen should be able to get their course fees paid for if they are studying A levels, OCR Nationals or an equivalent.

Correspondence courses

It is possible to do A levels and many other qualifications by correspondence course, although you may need to pay for this. Most funding for 16 to 18 year olds is linked to attendance at a state funded school or college. Remember to add up all the costs. In addition to the course fee you may have to pay for books, equipment, and taking the examination. Also factor in travel and accommodation if there are residential elements to the course.

Think carefully before your teen embarks on a course like this and ask about the sort of support they receive. Correspondence courses will suit those who are motivated enough to study by themselves. Check the Open and Distance Learning Quality Council website [**www.odlqc.org.uk**] for a list of accredited colleges and courses. Look at the different providers and compare what they offer.

> Matt is taking four AS levels. He is studying maths and English by distance learning, and attends college to study the more practically based physics and chemistry. As Matt is dyslexic, he has a scribe to support him in his college courses: he knows someone is there if he has not finished, which lowers his anxiety levels enabling him to perform well.
>
> Matt's mum Liz says, "Matt has studied at home, taken correspondence and online courses, and is now enjoying college life part-time too. Our approach to his education means he has had time to develop as a whole person, enjoy his childhood and become part of his local community, and the community of home educated families. I think he will stand out on his UCAS form as he has learnt how to learn and take a certain amount of responsibility for his learning from a young age."

In it for the long term

There are highs and lows in every sixth former's college career. It can help if you are forewarned about the low points. Everyone struggles when there are assessments and coursework to complete, mid-year exams, mocks and of course the end of year exams.

Study struggles

In the run-up to exams, parents get the chance to repeat the advice that it does help to study in advance, and sometimes a teen's active social life has to suffer. This can be particularly hard if exams come straight after Christmas when the rest of the family is relaxing.

If you can encourage your child through each set of challenges, they will work out what method of study works for them. Some people always leave everything to the last minute. If you think this description fits your teen, you may need to acknowledge that all your exhortations may not be able to change this.

> Louisa says, "When I had exams coming up, I didn't like people thinking I was trying too hard. Some nights I'd watch TV, even if mum and dad were reminding me to work, and then start studying once everyone else had gone to bed. I did a lot of my revision this way. It just suited me better."

For some teenagers it may be necessary to let them muck about and even fail mid-term examinations in order for them to realise how much work they need to put in. This can be a time when you need to bite your tongue and acknowledge the pressure your child is under. Provide chocolate biscuits, cups of tea and a listening ear if needed.

Money problems

There may be financial pressure on all the family if a 16 or 17 year old is still studying. The Education Maintenance Allowance (EMA) is available to teens in full-time study from families with income under a certain threshold and offers £10, £20 or £30 a week to help out with the costs like books, travel or equipment. There may also be bonuses for meeting targets set by school or college. It is still available even if your teen has a part-time job, and doesn't affect parents' benefits.

Most sixth forms and colleges also have Learner Support Funds, for students facing financial hardship, to help with emergencies, childcare costs, and accommodation costs if your teenager has to live away from home, travel costs and essential course-related equipment, materials and field trips. The student support or welfare officer at the college can help you and your child find out more about this fund.

Young parents and studying

There is also help available for young parents who want to study, under the Care to Learn scheme. If your daughter becomes pregnant during her course, both of you should talk to her college about her options. Depending on the timing and the college, she may need to take some time out, or choose to carry on studying part or full-time. The education department at the local education authority should also be able to help, and possibly arrange home tuition if necessary.

Care to Learn can help pay for childcare and travel costs while young parents are studying. It is available for full and part-time courses as well as learning through work. If you are looking for independent advice for teen parents-to-be, look up your local Brook Centre or similar young people's service where counsellors can help explore feelings and give impartial information.

Teen choices

In summary, the most important thing to remember is that most teenagers have reached the stage where they want to make their own choices. Try to look at your own expectations for your children and separate them from their desires. It can be painful and fruitless to try to force your teen into a career path, however worthy or in their best interests. Instead, help them to work out their interests, give them plenty of information, and draw on your reserves of patience while they spend a few years working out their future.

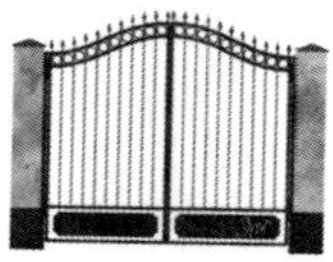

Conclusion

I hope if you have got this far you have some ideas, and can start helping your child who hates school. This book is not going to solve your child's problems on its own, but I hope it has shown you that you don't have to solve things by yourself either.

Almost every parent worries that they are doing a bad job at one time or another, especially if their child is unhappy. You are doing the best you can, with the resources you have. Make time to look after yourself, and share your worries with a friend or your partner. If you have internet access, take advantage of some of the many parenting forums to find another mum or dad who is going through the same thing, or who perhaps has found a solution.

Whatever the cause of your child's problems, it can help if you listen to them. Whatever their age, they will feel better for having talked about the issue. They may have some ideas of how to improve things too. If your child is at a stage where they won't talk to you, think about who else they respect: a family friend, relative, or older teen may be the outlet they need.

If your child has a problem at school, ask yourself, "Who can help?", and talk to a teacher, your GP, or someone at the local authority. You will find that there are many people with access to resources that you didn't even know about. A referral for extra help at school, or to a group for kids with similar issues, may make a real difference to your child.

Few children get through growing up without some problems, and school life can seem like a battle. There are ways through it, and I hope that you and your child can successfully navigate the current hurdle, and go on to enjoy life again.

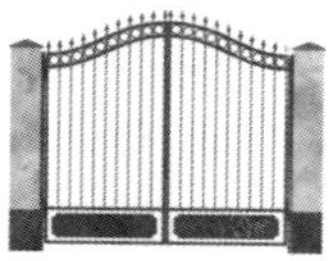